The Mentally Retarded in Society

The
Mentally Retarded
in Society

Stanley Powell Davies

with the collaboration of

KATHARINE G. ECOB

Columbia University Press, New York and London

Preface

THIS volume endeavors to present mental retardation in its social rather than its clinical aspects. It aims to show how various phases of public opinion and action have followed the evolution of scientific knowledge. The more recent trends of thought and action are particularly dealt with as indicating what a modern mental deficiency program might comprise.

The present work is built upon the work of the same author, *Social Control of the Mentally Deficient*, published in 1930, which followed a smaller volume entitled *Social Control of the Feebleminded*, published in 1923. It retains much of the historical and other pertinent material of the earlier volume, but has been expanded to include the many significant developments of later years and the changed thinking which brought them about.

The examples given of various services serve only as illustrations of work, which in many cases is conducted advantageously elsewhere. No attempt has been made to describe every service of every state, or to give an account of legislation not yet in effect. The emphasis is rather to trace, through the history of methods of care, the development of modern concepts.

My indebtedness to those who assisted in the preparation of earlier volumes is still great. For this edition, I acknowledge with gratitude the able assistance of many persons who gave generously of their time and thought to criticize the manuscript or aid in getting material. In particular, I would express great appreciation to Miss Katharine G. Ecob, whose collaboration has made this new edition possible. Miss Ecob has brought unique qualifications and sincere devotion to this task. As psychologist with the former New York State Commission on Mental Defectives, and later as executive secretary of the Committee on Mental Hygiene in the same state, Miss Ecob has made notable contributions to the understanding and treatment of mental retardation. Both through her work and her writings, she is a recognized leader in this field.

Stanley Powell Davies
October, 1958

Contents

Part One: Historical Background

I. *The Social Test of Mentality*

WHAT pictures from the literature of the past the very mention of the "feebleminded" conjures up! Menace to the progress of the race, root of social evils, burden of civilization—this was the way mental retardation used to be widely characterized. To no other form of human inadequacy have so many social blights been attributed: crime, delinquency, degeneracy, poverty, vagrancy, immorality, and their train. The truths and fallacies of these assertions, and the development of modern attitudes and programs are the subject of this book. Once considered a threat to the social order, those today known as retarded are now seen less as liabilities and more as potential assets, calling upon society not so much for control as for skilled help.

We must begin, first, by considering who the mentally retarded are. No one definition has been generally accepted, but there seems to be substantial agreement that the term contains three essential and interrelated concepts: (1) marked limitation of intelligence, which is due to (2) lack of normal development, rather than to mental disease or deterioration, and which manifests itself in (3) some degree of social and economic inadequacy. The terms retarded and mentally deficient are used interchangeably in this book, to include all who are described by the foregoing criteria.

We must note here the difficulties of formulating a precise definition. Intelligence can be measured with some accuracy. Social competence, on the other hand, for both the normal and the retarded, is susceptible of growth. It is always relative to the demands of the particular environment in which the individual functions. Thus, a retarded person will be less able to cope with unfavorable conditions than to manage himself in favorable conditions, such as living in a helpful home and in a neighborhood where work is plentiful.

Identification by Mental Age

The identification of the mentally deficient gave little difficulty in the days when only the grosser forms were recognized. It was with the discovery of the "moron" that problems of definition and identification arose. The recognition of the higher grades of retardation followed the invention and application of the Binet-Simon method of intelligence testing with its grading scale in terms of mental age, and later of intelligence quotient.

After considerable experience in applying the Binet-Simon scale to institutionalized patients, Dr. Henry H. Goddard, one of the first to introduce the work of Binet and Simon into this country, recommended in 1910 to the American Association for the Study of the Feebleminded a system of classification according to test ratings as follows: idiots, those with a mental age up to and including two years; imbeciles, those with a mental age of from three to seven years inclusive; morons, those with a mental age of from eight to twelve years.[1] This classification, adopted by the Association, unfortunately gave the general impression that all adults found by intelligence tests to have a mental age of twelve years or less were to be regarded as "feebleminded," although Dr. Goddard himself later explained that the upper level of mental deficiency was placed at twelve years because a survey of institutionalized patients showed that this mental age was the highest among these patients.

The terms idiot, imbecile, moron, are now less used, and the word feebleminded is becoming obsolete. The older terminology appears in this book only in reference to the work of the past, when it was in common use. Today the preferred terms are

[1] Goddard, "Feeblemindedness: A Question of Definition," *Journal of Psycho-Aesthenics*, 33:220.

severely, moderately, or mildly retarded, or low grade, middle grade, and high grade types. The changing terms reflect profound changes in thought. The basic problem is the same, but better understanding has shown it in an entirely different light.

Although some voices were raised to question Dr. Goddard's views prior to World War I, it was not until the results of the group psychological examinations of men recruited for the U.S. Army during World War I were published that the difficulties of this interpretation became generally manifest. Briefly, according to the official report, more than half of the drafted men were found to have mental ages of less than thirteen years, and thus would have been rated as subnormal according to the generally accepted classification. Many persons, hastily applying this figure to the general population, concluded that some 50,000,000 people in the country, or nearly half the population at the time, must presumably be mentally deficient! Taking into account the fact that many men of high intelligence selected as officers and for essential industries were not included in the examinations, and that certain qualifications should be made when test scores are interpreted, the fact remains that the Army examinations revealed a surprisingly large amount of what, by the standards then current, was regarded as mental deficiency. Prior to the publication of the Army results, most estimates placed the proportion of the mentally deficient in the general population at not more than 2 percent.

At first blush, these findings of the Army examinations were startling. After further thought, it became evident that there was patently something wrong with any classification that would serve to rate from one-sixth to one-half of the population as subnormal. The average intelligence is, after all, the norm.

Figures from World War II give a picture more in accordance with the modern view. The Selective Service System reported that of men rejected for service, some 4 percent were disqualified on grounds of what examiners classified as mental deficiency. National distribution, however, suggested that the rejections for mental deficiency as determined by the Selective Service were strongly influnced by regional differences in educational and cultural background.

Reliance upon the mental age criterion alone for classification is now generally recognized to have been inadequate and misleading. Other aspects of personality and behavior must be considered. The late Dr. Walter E. Fernald outlined ten different fields of inquiry as essential to study and diagnosis.[2] They were: physical examination, family history, personal and developmental history, school progress, examination in school work, practical knowledge and general information, social history and reactions, economic efficiency, moral reactions, mental examination. In this ten-fold inquiry, which for years was followed as a standard in clinical work, the intelligence test was only one of the ten points.

No sharp dividing line can be drawn between the subnormal and the normal simply because none exists. The mildly retarded on the one hand, and the dull normal on the other hand, do not represent wholly different groups of human beings, but rather a continuous series differing in degree but not in kind, and shading almost indistinguishably into one another. When the test of social competency is taken into account, who is retarded, and who is not, becomes a matter of relativity. Even Binet and Simon, in whose names so many unwarranted labels of deficiency have been applied on the basis of the intelligence rating alone, wrote as long ago as 1908: "A peasant, normal in ordinary surroundings of the fields, may be considered a moron in the city. In a word, retardation is a term relative to a number of circumstances which must be taken into account in order to judge each particular case."[3] Thus a countryman might appear subnormal in Paris because the competitive struggle in a highly urbanized environment requires a degree of intellectual keenness and of social adaptability not called for in a simple rural situation.

On a practical basis, a distinction can be observed between

[2] Fernald, "Standardized Fields of Inquiry for Clinical Studies of Borderline Defectives," *Mental Hygiene*, 1:211–34.

[3] Binet and Simon, *The Development of Intelligence in Children* (The Training School, Vineland, N.J.), pp. 266–67.

those of the retarded who are socially incompetent, and those who are reasonably adequate socially. Fully recognizing that there is no clear-cut dividing line between the socially competent and incompetent, just as there is no fixed dividing line in levels of intelligence, nevertheless, those who have social potentials do stand out from those with characteristics that make for social disability. Generally speaking, the latter group comes to public attention through the social difficulties they fall into, while the other group merges inconspicuously into the workaday world. The most effective programs seek by training and supervision to keep retarded persons from falling into social inadequacy.

Mental deficiency presents one of the largest and most challenging of social problems. Neglected, it will lead to manifold social difficulties; through modern measures shown to be practicable and fruitful, many of the retarded can find a useful and acceptable place in the social order.

II. *From Sorcery to Science*

A highly developed, complex, industrial civilization, demanding a great degree of application, specialization, and skill on the part of its working units, and making many and various social demands upon the individual, will reveal large numbers of persons unable to keep up with the social procession because of limited intelligence. In an earlier age, when the majority of the population lived a simple rural life and performed tasks requiring no high degree of training, the standard of mental competency was naturally much lower, with the result that only the more marked degrees of retardation were recognized as such. In these relative terms, mental deficiency constitutes a more conspicuous social problem today.

The more extreme degrees of deficiency have been recognized from early times. The Spartans dealt with the severely retarded in the sternest eugenic fashion, and obviously defective children are said to have been cast into the river or left to perish on the mountainside. The laws of Lycurgus countenanced the deliberate abandonment of "idiots," a practice which was probably followed to a certain extent throughout Greece, and according to Cicero, among the Romans also.

The Greek roots from which the word *idiot* is presumably derived are "iditas," a private person, or "idios," peculiar, that is, a person set apart or alone. Thus the roots contain the concept of nonsocial or extrasocial, the idea that these persons live in a world by themselves, and are more or less outside the pale of society. It was as such extrasocial beings that the mentally deficient for many centuries were commonly treated—shunned, ostracized, derided, persecuted, neglected—creatures considered incapable of human feeling, and therefore undeserving of human compassion.

The example and teachings of Christ as to the duty of mankind to the weak and helpless appear to have brought some alleviation to the lot of these unfortunates, and from that time on there were sporadic instances of the recognition of social responsibility for the care of the retarded. The Bishop of Myra (the Saint Nicholas of our Christmas time) in the fourth century is said to have shown particular compassion toward them, and to have urged giving them tender care. From the same motive, St. Vincent de Paul and his "Sisters of Charity," in the sixteenth century, gave kindly treatment to the retarded and other unfortunates whom they brought under care in the Bicêtre (famous hospital and asylum of Paris). In the Middle Ages, the mentally deficient frequently earned favor and support as fools and jesters of some noble master. In certain localities, they unwittingly received homage and reverence through the superstitious belief that they were "les enfants du bon Dieu," sacred beings having some mysterious connection with the unknown. Barr, writing in 1904, gave some examples of the latter treatment: "Proof of this commonly accepted belief that these creatures walked on earth but held their conversation in heaven is shown in the fact that Tycho Brahe had for his close companion a fool to whose mutterings the great astronomer listened as to a revelation. . . . In Brazil an imbecile in a family is considered more a joy than a sorrow; rich and poor alike roam the streets undisturbed, soliciting alms which are never refused; in this way among the poor an idiot may be the sole support of a family. The American Indian also allows these 'children of the Great Spirit' to go unharmed." [1]

Here reverence, there persecution, and all rooted in superstition! For the old abuse did not die out. The mental defective, regarded as a sacred being at one time and in one place, at another time and place was regarded as possessed by the evil spirit and subjected to all sorts of cruel indignities in the hope of exorcising

[1] Barr, *Mental Defectives*, p. 25.

the demon. As late as the days of the Reformation, Luther and Calvin regarded these mental incompetents as "filled with Satan."

The Savage of Aveyron

It was not until the beginning of the nineteenth century that the first educational and medical approach of a definitely scientific character was made to this problem. A party of sportsmen hunting in the woods of Caune, Aveyron, France, in 1798, came upon a wild creature of the human species, a boy of about eleven or twelve years, roaming naked through the woods like any animal, and feeding upon acorns and nuts. The hunters gave chase and captured the lad.

Bonaterre, Professor of Natural History in the Central School of the Department of Aveyron, took this boy under observation and described him as unused to our food, selecting his nourishment by smell, but at the same time indifferent to fragrant or foul odors; lying flat on the ground to drink; tearing garments placed upon him and trying constantly to escape; walking often on all fours; fighting with his teeth; giving few marks of intelligence; having no articulate language and even apparently devoid of the faculty of speech. It was later discovered that the boy's hearing was insensitive to loud noises and to music; yet he readily heard the fall of a nut. His sense of touch was likewise apparently deficient. As to sight, his eyes constantly wandered and could not be fixed on objects. Professor Bonaterre thought that "a phenomenon like this would furnish to philosophy and natural history important notions on the original constitution of man and on the development of his primitive faculties; *provided that the state of imbecility we have noticed in this child does not offer an obstacle to his instruction.*" [2]

Toward the end of the following year, 1799, the boy was taken to Paris for special observation and study. It was here that he came to the attention of Dr. Jean Itard, Chief Medical Officer of the National Institution for the Deaf and Dumb, where the

[2] Seguin, *Idiocy*, p. 16.

"Savage of Aveyron" was placed under care. Itard had been a devoted student of the famous Philippe Pinel, Physician-in-Chief of the Insane at the Bicêtre. Pinel, after observing the savage boy, was convinced of his idiocy,[3] and believed that being "affected with a malady to this time looked upon as incurable, he was not susceptible of any sort of sociability or instruction."

Itard was of the opinion that the boy was simply wild and entirely untaught. Therefore, he undertook what to others seemed a hopeless task, not with the object of improving or curing an idiot, but to "solve the metaphysical problem of determining what might be the degree of intelligence, and the nature of the ideas in a lad, who, deprived from birth of all education, should have lived entirely separated from the individuals of his kind."

Itard's hopes were doubtless founded on his familiarity with the remarkable results obtained in the training of deaf-mutes through the use of the methods of Pereire. It seemed to him that the boy had merely been deprived of normal social stimulation.

THE SCIENTIFIC APPROACH   Much interest centered about Itard's experiments with the boy, because it was thought that experimentation might shed light on the philosophical controversy of the day between two schools of thought, the nativists and the sensationalists. The former school assumed that the individual comes into the world with innate ideas which gradually unfold with the development of the mind. The sensationalists, to whom Itard adhered, as a follower of de Condillac, conceived of the mind as a "tabula rasa" waiting to receive all its impressions from the outside by the pathway of sensation. They held the view that all human faculty and knowledge are transformed sensation only.

It is interesting to note that de Condillac had sought to confirm his views by observations on a "wild boy," who was found living among the bears in the forests of Lithuania. As an exponent of sensationalism, Itard reasoned that he had merely to bring his

[3] The word idiocy was used at that time as the general term for mental deficiency.

"savage boy" to experience an ordered series of sensations in order to bring forth a normal intellectual and social being. Accordingly, Itard adopted the following program:

1. To endear him to social life, by making it more congenial than the one he was now leading; and . . . more like that he had but recently quitted.

2. To awaken his nervous sensibility, by . . . stimulants; and at other times by quickening the affections.

3. To extend the sphere of his ideas, by creating new wants.

4. To lead him to the use of speech.

5. To exercise the simple operations of his mind upon his physical wants.

For nine months Itard, with the aid of a competent matron, Madame Guerin, painstakingly applied to the young "savage" various measures calculated to carry this program into effect. At the end of that time, there was some concrete evidence of progress: (1) the boy's habits of sleeping and eating and of personal hygiene became more regular and more controlled; (2) his nervous sensibility increased so that the senses of touch, taste, and smell became more acute; (3) his circle of wants greatly increased, together with his affection for, and dependence upon, his governess; (4) speech was not attained, but whereas the boy had been entirely mute previously, he learned to give voice to certain monosyllables as *lait* (milk) and *O Dieu*, and finally, he acquired all the vowel sounds as well as d and l; (5) he learned to place objects together in proper order or sequence, such as placing together letters of the alphabet spelling *lait*.[4]

The scientific literature in the mental retardation field begins with the publication in 1801 of Itard's work, "De l'Education d'un Homme Sauvage," in which he described these first months of work with the savage boy.

Itard was not willing to relinquish his efforts with these slight evidences of progress, and apparently continued his work with the boy for about four years following the publication of his first report. The next report of his work was published in 1806

[4] Fynne, *Montessori and Her Inspirers* (New York, Longmans, 1924), p. 78.

and concludes the account of Itard's great experiment. Some time between the publication of his first and second reports, Itard reluctantly came to the conclusion that Pinel had been right in the first instance, and that the "Savage of Aveyron" was actually an idiot. It is said that when Itard was forced to admit the condition of idiocy because of the boy's limited ability to profit by education, he threw up his hands in a fit of despair and exclaimed: "Unfortunate! Since my pains are lost and my efforts fruitless, take yourself back to your forests and primitive tastes; or, if your new wants make you dependent on society, suffer the penalty of being useless, and go to Bicêtre, there to die in wretchedness!" [5] But this was only an outburst. A man of Itard's perseverance was not so quickly discouraged. Again he took up his Herculean task, but this time he adopted a modified program, simpler and better suited to the training of "the idiot in the savage."

EDUCATIONAL METHODS In his earlier attempts to educate Victor (as he had come to call the boy), Itard, believing that the boy was fundamentally normal and merely uncivilized, placed emphasis upon creating an environment that would call forth his normal self. Once he acknowledged the inherent defect in the lad, he addressed himself more directly to building up the physiological functions. It was with this in view that Itard outlined his new program as follows: (1) the development of the senses; (2) the development of the intellectual faculties; (3) the development of the affective functions.

In giving first attention to the development of the senses, Itard began with hearing and sight. By blindfolding the boy so that hearing would not be distracted by sight, he was successful in teaching him to distinguish gross differences in sound, as, for example, between a drum and a bell. Gradually, by leading him from greater differences to lesser ones, he taught him to recognize varying tones of his teacher's voice. After long training, the sense of sight was developed to the point where Victor could read slightly, that is, he was able to identify various written words,

[5] Seguin, *Idiocy*, p. 22.

although without understanding their meaning. He also learned to distinguish colors.

The sense of touch was next taken up. The boy learned to sense form and size so that by placing his hand in a bag of chestnuts and acorns, he could draw out an acorn or chestnut as directed. He also learned by touch alone to select certain block letters. The boy's sense of smell had already become acute as a result of Itard's earlier experiments with him. His sense of taste was likewise developed, so that he could differentiate between sweet and tart.

Itard expected a degree of mental development to follow directly upon this education of the senses, but he also undertook experiments specifically directed toward mental development. One of these disciplines consisted of learning to connect an object with its name through use, and such distinctions Victor was finally able to make. When certain verbs of action were written on the blackboard, Victor was taught to distinguish between them, and later was able to carry out the action indicated.

With so much progress, however, Itard was not content. The boy had not yet learned to speak. For over a year Itard gave special attention to the training of the vocal organs of his subject, in the hope of attaining this primary objective. In that he failed. Victor's speaking accomplishment did not go beyond uttering a few monosyllables. He was not much more than a mute even after all the painstaking training his devoted teacher had lavished upon him.

The period of puberty followed shortly and Itard hoped this would give a great stimulus to Victor's mental development. This change had the effect, however, of bringing out all the wild and uncontrollable elements in the boy. He gave way to violent outbursts of temper, and became so unmanageable that the authorities of the institution for the deaf and dumb, where Victor had continued to reside during his period of training, insisted that he be removed for the sake of other charges. Thus the first great educational project with a mental defective ended. Madame Guerin, who had been Victor's governess in the institution, and who had been Dr. Itard's indefatigable assistant, made a home for the boy outside of the institution, where he received kindly care until his death in 1828.[6]

Itard himself felt that his five years' labor had resulted in failure. The official opinion of the French Academy, as published in 1806, should, however, have been a source of comfort to him. It reads in part: "The Academy acknowledges that it was impossible for the institutor to put in his lessons, exercises, and experiments more intelligence, sagacity, patience, courage; and that if he has not obtained a greater success, it must be attributed, not to any lack of zeal or talent, but to the imperfection of the organs of the subject upon which he worked."

Itard gave no further time to his study after Victor passed from his hands. From his pioneer effort, however, can be traced in direct descent the scientific approach to mental deficiency. To prove, as Itard did, that the mentally retarded were capable of some degree of education, was a momentous contribution; it had all the zest of seeming to make something of nothing. But even more momentous was the inspiration which Itard imparted to a gifted pupil to devote his life to the understanding and training of this class of unfortunates. This pupil was Edouard Seguin.

[6] The best description of Itard's work the writer has found is contained in Fynne's *Montessori and Her Inspirers*. The writer would like to acknowledge his special indebtedness to this work.

III. *Seguin and American Beginnings*

EDOUARD Seguin, the first great teacher and leader in the mental deficiency field, was both physician and psychologist. In addition to having studied medicine and surgery under Itard, he had also been a pupil of the famous psychiatrist Esquirol. It was Esquirol who, writing in 1828, had formulated the first clear definition of what was then called idiocy as follows: "Idiocy is not a disease but a condition in which the intellectual faculties are never manifested or have never been developed sufficiently to enable the idiot to acquire such an amount of knowledge as persons of his own age, and placed in similar circumstances with himself are capable of receiving. Idiocy commences with life or at that age which precedes the development of the intellectual and affective faculties, which are from the first what they are doomed to be during the whole period of existence."

Seguin entered upon his life work full of idealism and love of humanity engendered by the teachings of Saint-Simon, of whose religious, political, and social thought he was an ardent follower. He championed the cause of the mentally handicapped as one of the most neglected of his day. As Esquirol expressed it, Seguin's mission was "the removal of the mark of the beast from the forehead of the idiot." [1]

Seguin, after studying the reports of Itard's work, recognized more fully than Itard himself had the significance of the results obtained. It was in the physiological method which Itard had begun to develop that Seguin thought he saw the secret of treatment and cure. He founded in Paris in 1837 the first successful school for the specific purpose of the education of idiots. Here

[1] Barr, *Mental Defectives*, p. 19.

his work was so productive that he was rewarded in 1842 with an appointment to the directorship of the enlarged school for idiots at the Bicêtre. He left the Bicêtre at the end of the year, however, and re-established his private school. His great work which stands as a classic landmark in the literature of mental deficiency, "The Moral Treatment, Hygiene, and Education of Idiots and Other Backward Children," published in 1846, was acclaimed by the French Academy and was commended by Pope Pius IX.

Seguin's program of physiological education was in practice a system of sensory-motor training accomplished by means of various ingenious methods which he devised. Seguin's theory of physiological education cannot be so simply expressed. He believed idiocy, i.e, mental deficiency, to be merely an isolation of the individual's mental life and personality, not an inherent or irremediable defect. This isolation he thought due to an infirmity of the nervous system which removes "the faculties of the child from under the control of the will, giving him up to the dominion of instinct." The awakening of the peripheral apparatus through training would establish contact with the outside world, awaken and develop the central nervous system, place the will in control, and unite the child with the moral world.[2]

The Physiological Method

Seguin gave primary credit for the development of the physiological method to the work of the French instructors of deaf-mutes and particularly to Jacob Rodrigues Pereire. His training program was stated by him as follows:

"The general training embraces the muscular, imitative, nervous, and reflective functions, susceptible of being called into play at any moment. All that pertains to movement, as locomotion, . . . prehension, manipulation, and palpation, by dint of strength, or exquisite delicacy; imitation and communication from mind to mind, through languages, signs, and symbols. . . . Then, from imitation is derived drawing; from drawing, writing; from

[2] Barr, *Mental Defectives,* p. 69.

writing, reading; which implies the most extended use of the voice in speaking, music, etc. . . . Let our natural senses be developed as far as possible, and we are not near the limits of their capacity. Then the instruments of artificial senses are to be brought in requisition; the handling of the compass, the prism . . . the microscope and others must be made familiar to all children, who shall learn how to see nature through itself, instead of through twenty-six letters of the alphabet; and shall cease to learn by rote, by trust, by faith, instead of by knowing." Seguin's physiological program fell into two main divisions: (1) the training of the muscles; (2) the training of the senses.

MOTOR TRAINING   The first task in motor training was to correct the automatic motions and supply the deficiencies of the muscular apparatus. Thus, subject to the particular needs of the individual, the training began with the overcoming of muscular incapacities and the development of various muscular movements. So far as possible, exercises common to the play of all children were relied upon, such as the use of the spade, the wheelbarrow, the wooden horse, the hammer, the ball. Seguin preferred such natural activities to more formal gymnastics.

As an essential first step in the development of motility, Seguin began by training the child to maintain voluntary immobility, because he believed that from positive immobility all action springs. After controlled immobility had been accomplished, the child was given training in walking. Different kinds of gymnastic equipment were used to induce this activity. If the legs did not bend, they were made to yield under the elasticity of a baby-jumper. If the feet did not come forward, placing the child on a spring-board often forced the desired response. Many other elaborate exercises were described by Seguin for the purpose of developing walking ability.

When this period of training had been successfully completed, training of the hand was taken up. One of the exercises outlined for training the hand in prehension (to seize, hold and let go) was that of climbing a ladder. The child who would not or could not grasp was placed with his feet on one round and his hands about another. If he did not keep hold of the round with his hands he was permitted to go through the sensation of falling (although saved from injury by a gymnastic belt). This process was continued until the child automatically held his grasp to keep from falling. Then the child was painstakingly taught to climb from round to round until the act of grasping became habitual.

SENSE TRAINING When the child completed the elaborate course for the development of the muscular system, the training of the senses was taken up. Seguin regarded the sense of touch as the most general of the senses, and, in fact, looked upon all the senses as being mere modifications of the sense of touch; therefore, he began with touch in the training of sensibility.

Hands that were so sensitive and delicate that they seemed to avoid normal contacts were made to come in touch with anything that was rough, such as in carrying bricks, turning coarse-handled cranks, spading, sawing. Hands that were too dull or insensitive were stimulated by being titillated with feathers, passed over slabs of marble, velvet, etc. Sometimes they were also plunged alternately into cold and warm water, or into bags filled with substances of differing consistency, such as eiderdown, peas, flour and small shot. The child then had to learn to tell the difference between the contents of the bags solely by means of touch. These examples merely serve to illustrate Seguin's system of training which he outlined in great detail.

Results of Seguin's Work

Seguin's work won wide recognition. Psychiatrists, including Esquirol and others, testified to the remarkable results he obtained. In 1844, a committee from the Paris Academy of Science critically examined his methods, and stated that he had undoubtedly solved the problem of idiot education. The methods he developed and the results he obtained furnished the principles of, and impetus to, organized efforts in behalf of the retarded in practically all of the European countries and in America. The published results of his work, together with the work of Dr.

Guggenbuhl, who conducted a successful school for cretins in Switzerland, and Dr. Saegert of the Asylum for Deaf Mutes in Berlin, were not long in prompting similar endeavors elsewhere.

In America many states had already established institutions for the care, treatment, and training of the blind, deaf-mutes, and the mentally ill. The mentally deficient, however, had been almost totally neglected, and those whose families were unable to provide for them had only the almshouse and the jail, with all the abuses that centered about these places in that day, left to them as a recourse.

Several attempts to educate retarded children in the institutions for the blind and deaf had met with more or less success. The most notable of these experiments was undertaken in 1839 by that remarkable man, pioneer in American work with the blind and deaf as well as with the mentally deficient, Dr. Samuel G. Howe, Director of the Perkins Institute for the Blind in Boston. Dr. Howe won fame in many directions. Among his achievements was the successful instruction of the blind deaf-mute, Laura Bridgman.

In 1842–43, Horace Mann and George Sumner visited the Bicêtre, observed Seguin's work, and became interested in it. The latter published an extended account of it in *Chambers' Journal*, where it came to the attention of Dr. Hervey B. Wilbur, of Massachusetts. Dr. Wilbur sent for Seguin's books, became enthusiastic about the work, and opened his home in Barre, Massachusetts, in July, 1848, as the first private school in this country for the education of the severely retarded.

AMERICA'S FIRST INSTITUTIONS The first official step to be taken in the direction of special state provision for the retarded was in New York in 1846 when Dr. F. P. Backus introduced in the legislature a bill providing for the establishment of a state asylum for idiots. This bill, however, was defeated at that session. In Massachusetts, legislative action directing an inquiry "into the condition of idiots in the Commonwealth" was taken in the same year. As an outcome of this inquiry, Massachusetts, on October 1, 1848, opened in South Boston, under the superintendency of Dr. Samuel G. Howe, an experimental school for the teaching of idiots. This was the first state institution for the mentally deficient to be established in this country. The institution was later moved to Waverley and is now known as the Walter E. Fernald State School.

In New York, the legislation proposed in 1846 was finally enacted in 1851, and in October of that year, a state school was opened at Albany with Dr. Hervey B. Wilbur as its first superintendent. In 1854 this school was transferred to Syracuse, where the first building in this country planned expressly for the education of mental defectives was erected. Dr. Seguin was present at the ceremonies attending the laying of the cornerstone, and evidently the occasion was a greatly moving one for him, for in his remarks he said: "God has scattered among us—rare as the possessors of genius—the idiot, the blind, the deaf-mute, in order to bind the rich to the needy, the talented to the incapable, all men to each other, by a tie of indissoluble solidarity. The old bonds are dissolving; man is already unwilling to continue to contribute money or palaces for the support of the indolent nobility; but he is every day more ready to build palaces and give annuities for the indigent or infirm, the chosen friends of our Lord Jesus. See that cornerstone—the token of a new alliance between humanity and a class hitherto neglected—that, ladies and gentlemen, is your pride; it is the greatest joy of my life; for I, too, have labored for the poor idiot." [3] The Syracuse institution remains today on its original site as a part of the New York system and is known as the Syracuse State School.

In 1852 a private school for mental defectives was established in Germantown, Pennsylvania. In 1854 the state began the policy of partial support of this institution, which it has since maintained. In 1855 the school was moved to Philadelphia, and in 1859 it was located at Elwyn.

Ohio followed with the opening of an institution at Columbus in 1857. In Connecticut in the following year a private but state-aided institution was opened at Lakeville. This was later taken

[3] Fourth Annual Report, Syracuse State School, p. 43.

over by the state and closed when the state institution for this class was established at Mansfield. By 1890 fourteen states were maintaining separate state institutions for mental defectives. In 1904 the number of state institutions had increased to 21, in 1910 to 26, in 1923 to 40. By 1958 only one state was without an institution for the retarded.

This early work for the retarded, particularly in Massachusetts, New York and Pennsylvania, was materially aided by the personal presence of the master, Edouard Seguin. Seguin's deep interest in social problems had led him to take an active part in the political affairs of France, and during the revolutionary days of 1848 he was unable to hold aloof. He had been an active supporter of Louis Napoleon when the latter was seeking recognition by the French people, and continued to support him when he was elected Prince President of the republic. When, in 1850, it was evident that this new Napoleon was proving disloyal to his original supporters, Seguin voluntarily exiled himself from his homeland, and came with his wife and young son to live in the United States. With the exception of occasional visits to Europe, he spent the rest of his days in this country.

At the invitation of Dr. Samuel G. Howe, Superintendent of the recently opened Massachusetts School for the Feebleminded, Dr. Seguin's first months in this country were spent at that institution advising in the organization of its work. Later Dr. Seguin rendered invaluable service in helping Dr. Hervey B. Wilbur organize the new school for the mentally retarded at Syracuse. Subsequently, he served for a period as head of the Pennsylvania School for Idiotic and Feebleminded Children in Philadelphia. Seguin also personally assisted in the organization of the institutions in Ohio and Connecticut, and the former New York City institution on Randall's Island. It was while in this country that Seguin published his most widely read work, "Idiocy and Its Treatment by the Physiological Method." Early in 1880, he opened a private school for mental defectives in New York City, but died in October of that year. Following his death, his wife took charge of this school and moved it to East Orange, N.J., where it was in operation for many years.

THE HOPE OF CURING IDIOCY All these early schools for the retarded were organized in the hope of largely overcoming, if not entirely curing, mental retardation by the application of the physiological method, and of so greatly improving the condition of patients that they could be returned to the community, capable of self-guidance and of earning an independent livelihood. These schools were, therefore, frankly educational institutions.

In his first report as Superintendent of the Syracuse institution Dr. Wilbur wrote: "We do not propose to create or supply faculties absolutely wanting; nor to bring all grades of idiocy to the same standard of development . . . nor to make them all capable of sustaining creditably all the relations of a social and moral life; but rather to give to *dormant* faculties the greatest practicable development and to apply those awakened faculties to a useful purpose under the control of an aroused and disciplined will."

Gradually, however, it became clear that severe retardation was not curable or even greatly improvable. The emphasis was placed, therefore, upon receiving children of higher-grade type.

What were the results accomplished by these early training schools? From our knowledge of this problem today, we may be sure that no case of mental retardation was cured. In other words, the best efforts of the best trained physicians and teachers were unable, by the physiological or any other method, to make up the intellectual lack which handicapped the child. Improvements in physical and muscular development, in habits, in behavior, in self-help, and in occupational ability were realized in many cases. The children admitted for training, while not curable as regards their intellectual defect, were teachable and they profited by the physiological method to the extent of their limited endowments.

The improvement shown, however, was frankly not nearly so great as had been originally anticipated. Only a very small proportion of the pupils could be returned to the community, even after years of training, on a self-supporting basis. This changed the aspect of the whole problem. It created an unforeseen difficulty. It had not been intended, when these schools were organized, that the state should assume indefinite custodial care of these cases. The state was simply to educate them by a special method during the regular school period. Now the institutions found themselves besieged on two sides. The parents of the children who had completed the regular course of training and who theoretically should have been ready to return to the community begged that these boys and girls (now young men and women) be retained in the institution because of their obvious dependency. On the other hand, there was an even greater demand from all sides for the admission of new cases of all ages and all types. It became more and more evident that the state must squarely face the large and less hopeful problem of providing indefinite custodial care for a growing number of cases.[4]

CUSTODIAL CARE So the idea of the institution as an educational project pure and simple had to be abandoned. More and more it was recognized that the state would have to enlarge its institutional accommodations to make provision for thousands of the retarded.

The Syracuse institution continued its policy of receiving mentally deficient children of school age capable of being benefited by instruction. In 1870, New York City organized its own hospital and school on Randall's Island, where it received all types of cases. In 1878, the state opened a separate branch of the Syracuse state institution at Newark, N.Y., to meet the problem of custodial care for subnormal women of child-bearing age. In 1885, the institution at Newark was separately incorporated. The further needs of custodial care for all ages and both sexes, and especially for low-grade and delinquent cases, led to the opening in 1894 of the Rome State Custodial Asylum at Rome, N.Y. Other states, likewise, were forced to follow the

[4] Fernald, "History of the Treatment of the Feebleminded," *Proceedings of the 20th National Conference Charities and Correction* (Chicago, 1893).

same course, and for many years following the death of Seguin, the custodial aspect was uppermost in the State institutions.

SEGUIN'S LASTING CONTRIBUTION   Although the early promise of Seguin's work was not fulfilled, and the application of his methods did not succeed in curing a single case of retardation, nevertheless, his devoted and painstaking service to those so afflicted did not go for naught. Seguin himself emphasized that his methods were applicable equally to normal and to retarded children. The great influence of his work upon educational practice with normal children is notably exemplified in the Montessori system of sensory and motor training. Maria Montessori, the founder of that movement, freely credited Seguin with the chief inspiration for her work. While it cannot be said that the work of John Dewey and later leaders in the modern educational movement was the direct outcome of Seguin's work, it is nonetheless true that Seguin, far in advance of his own time, distinctly represented some of the best thought and practice in education today.

Today in America there are many progressive institutions that have carried on under the inspiration of Seguin, and that have not been content with anything less than developing every child, no matter how handicapped, to his own highest possible level. Their aim has been to make each child capable of the greatest possible degree of self-help, agreeable in habits and behavior, and sufficiently able to use muscles and senses to keep himself happily occupied at work or play.

Thus, the nineteenth century witnessed a promising beginning of organized scientific work in behalf of the retarded, saw the development of a sound educational program, brought defeat of the hope of curing retardation, marked the establishment of state institutions, and secured recognition of social responsibility for dealing with this problem.

IV. An Invention and a Discovery

JUST as the dawn of the nineteenth century had witnessed the first scientific attempt to educate a person afflicted with mental deficiency and to arrive at an understanding of this condition, so the beginning of the twentieth century saw a general public awakening to mental deficiency as a social problem of the first magnitude. The two factors mainly responsible for this rather suddenly aroused and widespread concern about a problem which had previously existed without any general public notice were: (1) the development and application of the Binet-Simon method of intelligence testing; and (2) the development of the eugenics movement, together with the rediscovery of the Mendelian laws of heredity, and resulting heredity studies.

The work of Dr. Alfred Binet and Dr. Théodore Simon, who originated a method of measuring intelligence, deserves to rank with that of Seguin as an epoch-making contribution to the understanding and treatment of retardation. To France goes the credit for the brilliant achievement of Binet and Simon, as it does for the pioneer work of Itard and Seguin in behalf of the retarded, for Pinel's great courage in ushering in the dawn of a new day for the mentally ill, for Pereire's notable invention of the oral method of training the deaf, and for Haüy's inauguration of the embossed system of type and of organized instruction for the blind.

Alfred Binet, the son of a physician, and himself a student of medicine, was drawn toward experimental psychology before the completion of his medical course. In 1889 he established at the Sorbonne the first psychological laboratory in France. Théodore Simon took his degree in medicine at Paris, and later became physician at the mental hospital at Saint-Yon. Binet's psychological studies led him to take a special interest in abnormal children and he spent many years in the study of retarded and unstable children in public institutions of Paris, and also of normal and retarded children in the primary schools. As a result of this interest, he was appointed, in 1904, a member of a commission charged with the "Study of Measures to be Taken, Showing the Benefits of Instruction for Defective Children." This commission decided that no child suspected of retardation should be transferred from the regular school to a special class except on certification that because of the state of his intelligence he was unable to profit from instruction in the regular classes. But the commission did not indicate how the examination of each child should be made.

Binet was appointed director of the work and was charged with the problem of devising a system for the examination and grading of the children. In this work he associated with him Dr. Simon. Up to that time there existed great variation and confusion among authorities as to the classification of individual cases of mental deficiency. This, as Binet indicates, was due partly to lack of uniformity in terminology and partly to ignorance or carelessness. Even well-trained physicians using the same terminology constantly disagreed in the diagnosis and classification of the same child. This was fundamentally because the physician made his diagnosis of the child on the basis of his own subjective impression. What Binet sought, therefore, was a "precise basis for differential diagnosis" to be obtained by objective methods.

The system devised by Binet and Simon to meet this need was called by them "a measuring scale of intelligence." This scale was composed of a series of tests of increasing difficulty, starting from the lowest intellectual level that can be observed and ending with that of average intelligence.

The Invention of Intelligence Testing

Binet distinguished between native intelligence and acquired instruction and sought to measure natural and general intelligence apart from instruction. He tried each test on a large number of normal children grouped according to chronological age. The most advanced in the series of tests which the large majority of children of a given chronological age could answer satisfactorily was regarded as indicating the normal mental level of a child of that age. If the majority of children at a given age failed in a given test, he tried it on older children. In this way the scale drawn up was based on actual experiment with a large number of cases. Accordingly the unit of measurement came to be mental age, that is, the chronological age at which the average child might be expected to pass the mental test corresponding to that age. Thus the retarded child would fall some years short of passing the test for his chronological age, while the superior child would be able to pass tests devised for the average child older than himself. This method for the first time established a psychological criterion of mental deficiency to supplement the medical and pedagogical criteria to which Binet gave due recognition. As first published in 1905, Binet outlined a series of thirty objective tests arranged in order of difficulty, but not yet assigned to definite years. These 1905 tests fell into disuse following the publication of his later work. In 1908 the scale with the grading by years was published in "L'Année Psychologique." This is the most complete statement of Binet's system of intelligence measurement.

Binet's 1905 tests reached America in 1906, but attracted little attention. In the fall of that year, the Research Laboratory at The Training School at Vineland, N.J. was established with Dr. Henry H. Goddard as director. In the spring of 1908, Dr. Goddard made a visit to Europe in the interests of research, and there first learned of the Binet tests. Upon his return to Vineland, Dr. Goddard, although highly skeptical as to the practical value of the scale, tried it on the boys and girls at Vineland, and was surprised to find that the classification of the children, according to the results of the Binet test, corresponded closely with their grading according to institutional experience. Dr. Goddard thereupon became the leading exponent of the tests in this country.

In 1908, he published a brief account of the 1905 tests and in 1910, an abstract of the 1908 scale. Binet died in 1911. In 1916, with the permission of Dr. Simon, a complete translation of the Binet-Simon 1908 article was published by The Training School under the title "The Development of Intelligence in Children." Later in the same year a companion volume was published, giving a translation of Binet and Simon's work, "The Intelligence of the Feebleminded."

THE TESTS IN AMERICA It was through Dr. Goddard's sponsorship that the Binet-Simon scale gained wide currency, both in this country and in all parts of the world and became, with modifications and adaptations, the standard method of classifying the retarded according to intelligence levels. Dr. Walter E. Fernald paid tribute to the epoch-making research and studies of Goddard at Vineland and his inspired recognition of the vast significance of Binet's theory and technique for the measurement of variations of human intelligence. Goddard made the Binet tests practical, applied them to thousands of normal and retarded children and so interpreted the results that the world will forever be his debtor.

As to the tests themselves, Dr. Fernald said, "The theory and practice of mental testing and the discovery of the concept of mental age did more to explain feeblemindedness, to simplify its diagnosis, and to furnish accurate data for training and education, than all the previous study and research from the time of Seguin." [1]

In this country, Dr. Henry H. Goddard, and also Dr. F. Kuhlmann of the Minnesota School for the Feebleminded at Faribault, performed the first service of translating the Binet-Simon scale, and of adapting it to American children. Later, Drs. Terman, Yerkes, Bridges, Hardwick, and others extended and revised the scale and introduced improved methods of scoring. Dr. Terman's revision, the Stanford Scale, made the tests much more usable and the scoring more accurate. The Binet Scale gave the measure of intelligence only in terms of mental age, which im-

[1] Fernald, *Journal of Psycho-Aesthenics*, 29:209.

plied a varying degree of deficiency or superiority, depending upon the chronological age. The introduction of the intelligence quotient remedied this defect, since it is simply the ratio of actual age to mental age, obtained by dividing the latter by the former.

Terman's classification of intelligence quotients is as follows: [2]

I.Q.	*Classification.*
Above 140	"Near" genius or genius.
120–140	Very superior intelligence.
110–120	Superior intelligence.
90–110	Normal, or average, intelligence.
80– 90	Dullness, rarely classifiable as feeblemindedness.
70– 80	Border-line deficiency, sometimes classifiable as dullness, often as feeblemindedness.
Below 70	Definite feeblemindedness.

Such were the beginnings of intelligence tests. They have since been greatly improved by revision and extension and by the development of performance tests which are independent of language. It may fairly be said that intelligence tests, limited though their use may be, were the starting point of the modern projective techniques for the study of personality.

THE EXTENT OF MENTAL RETARDATION   As a measuring instrument, the Binet tests furnished for the first time a means of determining the extent of retardation in the general population. Practically speaking, it was impossible to put the entire population through this measuring process, but studies of various population "samples," regarded as representative, formed the basis of estimates.

The best opportunity for general intelligence testing was afforded in the public schools. One of the earliest of such studies was made by Dr. Goddard of 2,000 children comprising an entire public school system. From this study, Dr. Goddard concluded that 2 percent of school children "are so mentally defective as to preclude any possibility of their ever being made normal

[2] L. M. Terman, *The Measurement of Intelligence* (Boston, Houghton Mifflin, 1916).

and able to take care of themselves as adults." Dr. Goddard later applied this scale to a number of children in the New York public schools, and from his findings there, he was convinced that 2 percent was a safe figure.[3]

Other public school surveys made by other examiners resulted in percentages of mentally deficient children found, ranging from one-half of 1 percent to 2 percent, the varying results being accounted for by differences in the methods and standards of the examiners. Dr. Kuhlmann came to the conclusion that the number of retarded children in the schools was not much, if any, over 1 percent. The most convincing and the most generally accepted evidence on this point was that of Dr. Terman, based on a study of 1,000 unselected children in various schools in western states. Dr. Terman found that 2.3 percent of these school children had intelligence quotients under 75, and therefore, according to his classification, were either borderline or definitely deficient. Two percent has been generally recognized by school authorities as a reliable figure for planning.

The Discovery of the "Moron"

The refinements of the intelligence tests were responsible for bringing to light a very large group of persons of borderline intelligence who were hitherto largely unrecognized as retarded. They were individuals whose intelligence quotients registered above the upper level of the "imbecile" group and below what was considered to be the lower level of normal intelligence. To designate this class of high grade and borderline mental defectives, Dr. Goddard suggested the term "moron," from the Greek word meaning foolish.

Prior to World War I, few community studies to determine the prevalence of mental deficiency in the general population had been made. The supreme opportunity to measure the intelligence of a large proportion of the country's population came during the war when these tests could be given to the troops in

[3] *School Training of Defective Children* (New York, World, 1914).

various army encampments. The results of the tests and the various estimates of the general extent of mental deficiency in the population based on them have already been noted. Even when most conservatively interpreted, the army tests revealed a much larger number of persons below what had generally been accepted as the average level of intelligence than had previously been suspected.

The "moron" was an alarming discovery. Surveys indicated that thousands of his kind were to be found among the general population, generally unrecognized for what they were, and with practically no facilities for their training. Institutional care for more than a small fraction was out of the question since the number of institutional beds was ridiculously small compared with the legions of the retarded. "What shall be done with the moron?" became the almost universal query.

v. Eugenic Alarms

WHILE these revelations of the wide extent of mental deficiency in the community were being made, other studies were indicating that the subnormal tend almost invariably to reproduce and multiply their kind in ever growing numbers. Public attention was consequently directed toward the eugenic aspects of the problem.

Sir Francis Galton was the father of the eugenics movement. As early as 1865 he had put forward the idea that systematic efforts should be undertaken to improve the human breed by checking the birth rate of the unfit and furthering the productivity of the fit. Sir Francis coined the word eugenic (well born) and used it for the first time in his work on "Inquiries Into Human Faculty and Its Development," published in 1883. He defined eugenics as "the science which deals with all influences that improve the inborn qualities of a race." The eugenics movement is generally regarded as dating, however, from the publication in *Nature* in 1901 of Sir Francis Galton's paper on "Possible Improvement of the Human Breed." In the preceding year the botanists De Vries, Correns, and Tschermark, by independent investigations, verified and brought to light the long-forgotten Mendelian principle of heredity. Stimulated by the fast growing interest in eugenics, it was not long before researchers began to apply the Mendelian theory to the transmission of human characters and among them mental retardation.

Heredity as an etiological factor in mental deficiency had been recognized in a general way among early students of this problem but it was considered as one of many factors and not of predominant importance. Nor was the mode of transmission of the defect understood.

"Royal" Lines of Degeneracy

The revived interest in the question of the transmissibility of mental defect that sprang up in connection with the eugenics movement led to various studies of the family histories of certain supposedly defective stocks. These studies furnished a mass of data that was widely accepted as concrete evidence that mental deficiency is strongly and preponderantly hereditary. One such study, which had been made many years previously by a student of penology, and which purported to show the combined influence of heredity and environment in the production of crime, was brought to light and reviewed from the standpoint of mental deficiency. This was Robert L. Dugdale's study of "The Jukes," which had been first published in 1877. This work was reprinted in 1910.

The Dugdale study included the progeny of five notorious sisters of whom the most notorious was known as "Margaret, the mother of criminals." There were 709 individuals included in this study, of whom 540 were of Juke blood and 169 were of "X" blood connected by marriage or cohabitation. Of these 709, Dugdale stated there were 180 who had either received poor-house care or out-door relief aggregating 800 years. Among the social offenders were listed 140 criminals and other law-breakers, 60 habitual thieves, 50 common prostitutes, and 40 women venereally diseased. Dugdale estimated that the total cost to the state resulting from the socal failures of this one stock over a period of 75 years amounted to $1,308,000. Although Dugdale reported only one case of outright deficiency, one of mental disease and one of epilepsy in the Juke blood, it was generally assumed by those who studied the reprinted work that the degeneracy of this stock was a mere reflection of an hereditary taint of mental deficiency passed down from generation to generation by inbreeding within an isolated environment. A verification of this assumption was sought in a later study made by Arthur H. Estabrook of the former Eugenics Record Office entitled, "The Jukes in 1915." After a comprehensive investigation Estabrook concluded, "One-half of the Jukes were and are feebleminded, mentally incapable of responding normally to the expectations of society," and further, "all of the Juke criminals were feebleminded."

A study similar to that of the Jukes, and inspired by Dugdale's work, was made by the Rev. O. C. McCullough in Indiana, and published in 1888 under the title, "The Tribe of Ishmael." It added further data in support of the role of heredity in multiplying degenerate and mentally deficient stocks.

In 1910, Dr. Henry H. Goddard read a paper before the American Breeders Association,[1] in which he presented charts of the family histories of a number of patients of the Vineland institution showing the presence of mental defect, generation after generation. These charts were presented by Dr. Goddard without comment or conclusion, but in themselves strongly suggested the transmission of defect in the typical Mendelian way.

Dr. Charles B. Davenport in his work on *Heredity in Relation to Eugenics,* published in 1911, accepted these earlier charts of Dr. Goddard as the basis for formulating the following conclusions with regard to the heredity of mental deficiency: "There are laws of inheritance of general mental ability that can be sharply expressed. Low mentality is due to the *absence* of some factor, and if this factor that determines normal development is lacking in both parents, it will be lacking in all of their offspring. *Two mentally defective parents will produce only mentally defective offspring.* This is the first law of inheritance of mental ability. . . . The second law of heredity of mentality is that, aside from 'Mongolians,' probably no imbecile is born except of parents who, if not mentally defective themselves, both carry mental defect in their germ plasm." Thus Davenport gave the first definite statement of the heredity of mental deficiency in terms of the Mendelian formula.

THE "GOOD-BAD" FAMILY In 1912 Dr. Goddard published his history of *The Kallikak Family,* which has become the best known and most widely quoted of all the studies of defective

[1] "Heredity in Feeblemindedness," *American Breeders Magazine,* 1:165-78.

stock. In the preface to this study Dr. Goddard himself is somewhat cautious in drawing conclusions. He states: "To the scientific reader we would say that the data here presented are, we believe, accurate to a high degree. It is true that we have made rather dogmatic statements and have drawn conclusions that do not seem scientifically warranted from the data. . . . The reference to Mendelism is an illustration of what we mean. It is, as it is given here, meager and inadequate and the assumption that the given law applies to human heredity is an assumption so far as the data presented are concerned."

The Kallikak family was traced back through Deborah Kallikak, a girl of deficient mentality, who was an inmate of the Vineland institution at the time of the study. The name of Kallikak is doubtless one of the best known of fictitious names. It may be freely translated as the "good-bad" family. Such a family it appears to have been. With the assistance of Miss Elizabeth S. Kite, a research historian, the progenitors of Deborah were traced back a number of generations to Martin Kallikak Sr., of Revolutionary War days, who was of a reputedly "good old family," and of perhaps better than average mentality.

When Martin Sr. was about twenty, the Revolutionary War began, and he straightway "joined up" with the Colonial forces. At an inn, he met a girl, presumed to be subnormal, who subsequently gave birth to a boy of whom Martin Sr. was the reputed father. In any event, the boy was named by the mother after Martin Sr., and thus, as Dr. Goddard puts it, "has been handed down to posterity the father's name and the mother's mental capacity." For Martin Kallikak Jr., the great-great-grandfather of Deborah (the Vineland patient), inherited his mother's retardation, according to Dr. Goddard's history, and became the ancestor of 480 descendants, of whom 143 proved to be subnormal, while only forty-six were regarded as normal. The rest were unknown or doubtful. Included in these 480 descendants, according to Dr. Goddard, were: 36 illegitimate; 33 sexually immoral, mostly prostitutes; 24 confirmed alcoholics;

3 epileptics; 3 criminals; 8 keepers of houses of prostitution; 82 who died in infancy.

How could Dr. Goddard and his field workers determine that these departed ancestors of Deborah were mentally deficient? To that Dr. Goddard answered: "Some record or memory is generally obtainable of how the person lived, how he conducted himself, whether he was able to make a living, how he brought up his children, what was his reputation in the community; these facts are frequently sufficient to enable one to determine, with a high degree of accuracy, whether the individual was normal or otherwise. Sometimes the condition is marked by the presence of other factors. For example, if a man was strongly alcoholic, it is almost impossible to determine whether he was also feebleminded, because the reports usually declare that the only trouble with him was that he was always drunk, and if he had been sober, he would have been all right. This may be true, but on the other hand, it is quite possible that he was feebleminded also."

As to the "good" branch of the family, Martin Sr., after getting his honorable discharge, made a respectable marriage and thus started another line of descendants of a contrasting sort. On this legitimate side of the family, all of the 496 direct descendants turned out to be normal people. Two of the men were alcoholic, another sexually delinquent, but even these three black sheep were not mentally defective, so the history states. The descendants of this union stood out as highly respected and leading citizens and have in every way been assets instead of liabilities to the community.

The Kallikak findings brought Dr. Goddard to this conclusion: "Feeblemindedness is hereditary and transmitted as surely as any other character." Following the publication of his Kallikak study, that conclusion seems to have been quite generally accepted by students of social problems.

Many other similar studies of family histories have been made. Among the best known are: "The Zero Family" by Joerger,

1908; *The Nam Family* by Arthur H. Estabrook, 1912; "The Hill Folk" by Davenport and Danielson, 1912; "The Pineys" by Elizabeth S. Kite, 1913; "The Jukes in 1915" by Arthur H. Estabrook, 1915; "The Family of Sam Sixty" by Mary S. Kostir, 1916; "Dwellers in the Vale of Siddem" by A. C. Rogers and Maud A. Merrill, 1918. Practically all of these studies give support to the same conclusion: the hereditary transmission of mental defect in substantial accordance with the Mendelian formula.

Studies of Heredity

In his larger work, *Feeblemindedness, Its Causes and Consequences*, published in 1914, Dr. Goddard affirmed more definitely than in his earlier writings his conviction of the hereditary nature of a large proportion of retardation and of the Mendelian mode of its transmission. This work gave the results obtained from a study of institutional cases at Vineland. Goddard said, after studying the offspring of 324 matings: "Since our figures agree so closely with Mendelian expectation . . . the hypothesis seems to stand: viz., normal-mindedness is, or at least behaves like, a unit character; is dominant and is transmitted in accordance with the Mendelian law of inheritance."

Several English authorities, notably Tredgold and Lapage, agreed with these American findings; in fact, their estimates of the proportion of hereditary cases exceeded the American figures, and were placed at 90 percent. Their conception of the hereditary process, however, was somewhat at variance with the prevailing American view. Both Tredgold and Lapage were unable to find evidence that retardation is largely inherited in the strict sense of the word, that is, from retardation in the ancestry, resulting from the absence in the germ plasm of a determiner for normality. The early studies of these English authorities rather led them to the conclusion that retardation is more often the expression in the offspring of *various* forms of mental deviations in the ancestors, rather than of deficiency alone. For example, Dr. Tredgold said: "In my experience it is commoner for the ancestors of defectives to suffer from such conditions as insanity, epilepsy, dementia, and allied psychopathological states, than it is for them to be actually mentally deficient." [2]

The first large-scale systematic survey of the care of the retarded was that undertaken by the British Royal Commission in 1904. The report of this Commission in eight volumes was published in 1908. In its four years of investigation, the Commission examined 248 expert witnesses. It also appointed medical inspectors to make personal investigations of conditions in sixteen separate typical districts, rural and urban.

The evidence was summed up by the Commissioners as follows: "That both on the grounds of fact and of theory there is the highest degree of probability that feeblemindedness is usually spontaneous in origin—that is, not due to influences acting on the parent—and tends strongly to be inherited." [3]

Fecundity of the Retarded

Coupled with these findings as to heredity was the sweeping generalization widely accepted on very limited and incomplete evidence and frequently broadcast by writers on population questions, that the subnormal reproduce at a much more rapid rate than normal stocks, and that this differential birth rate threatens to overwhelm civilization. For example, Stoddard, citing as evidence the heredity studies referred to above, wrote under the heading, "The Nemesis of the Inferior":

"Feeblemindedness is a condition characterized by such traits as dull intelligence, low moral sense, lack of self-control, shiftlessness, improvidence, etc. It is highly hereditary, and unfortunately it is frequently associated with great physical strength and vitality, so that feebleminded persons usually breed rapidly, with no regard for consequences. In former times the numbers of the feebleminded were kept down by the stern processes of natural

[2] A. F. Tredgold, *Mental Deficiency*, 4th ed. (New York, Wood, 1922).
[3] *An Abstract of the Report to the Royal Commission on the Care and Control of the Feebleminded*, p. 24.

selection, but modern charity and philanthropy have protected
them and have thus favored their rapid multiplication." [4]

Dr. Tredgold was frequently quoted in support of the greater
fecundity of the retarded. In 1910, he stated: "It is quite clear,
therefore, that the number of children born of feebleminded
women throughout the country must be very considerable, and
when we remember how strongly hereditary this condition is,
and how exceedingly probable it is that these children will grow
up, if not actually mentally defective, at any rate, paupers, prostitutes, criminals or ne'er-do-wells, we see how serious must be
the consequences of this propagation upon the future of the nation. . . . As is well-known, the birth rate of the country is
steadily declining; but this decline is not general, it is selective,
and unfortunately the selection is in the wrong direction." [5] The
conclusion reached by the British Royal Commission was to the
same effect.

Dr. Goddard gave data on the number of children born to 287
mothers of children then in the Vineland institution. These data,
classified according to the type of retardation in the child under
care, indicated an average of 7.1 children in the hereditary group. [6]

On such evidence, plus newspaper headlines, were based the
many alarming assertions as to the social dangers involved in the
rapid rate of reproduction of mentally defective stocks. Consideration of this and more recent evidence, and also of the question
of the heredity of mental deficiency, is reserved for a later
chapter.

The revelations of the early years of the new century with
regard to mental deficiency were of a most disturbing kind.
Combined with evidence purporting to show the strongly hereditary nature of mental defect were the further findings as to the
rapid rate of multiplication of the mentally unfit and the extent
of uncontrolled mental deficiency in the community. All these
revelations were responsible for bringing the problem of mental

[4] L. Stoddard, *Revolt Against Civilization* (New York, Scribner's, 1922).
[5] *Contemporary Review* (June, 1910), pp. 720–21.
[6] H. H. Goddard, *Kallikak Family* (New York, Macmillan, 1912), p. 473.

deficiency out of its institutional seclusion into the glare of social notoriety. The eugenic and social alarms did not fall on deaf ears. The nation was aroused. The hunt began. The more thoroughly the mental defective was searched for and found, the more completely was he apparently involved in all manner of offenses against the social order. The social indictment found in the case of the Mental Defective vs. Society will be reviewed in the following chapter.

VI. The Social Indictment

THE findings of the hereditary character, the rapid multiplication, and the wide prevalence of mental deficiency were of special moment in the light of the supposed social shortcomings of the mentally handicapped. Prior to the opening of the twentieth century when mental defectives were thought of in terms of the lower-grade cases, the question of the antisocial conduct of the mentally deficient had scarcely received attention. The irresponsibility of certain types was apparent, to be sure, but the ready recognition of the severely retarded and the comparatively small number of such cases facilitated the necessary custodial care and supervision. It will be recalled, for example, that by the standards of his day, Dugdale noted only one case of deficiency, among all the Jukes of his study; by the standards of 1915, Dr. Estabrook found that "one-half of the Jukes were and are feebleminded." Thus what was regarded in 1877 as primarily a problem of criminal degeneracy, became in 1915 primarily a problem of mental deficiency. How these ideas became modified is discussed in later chapters.

The report of the British Royal Commission in 1908 was the first comprehensive study to reveal the close connection between retardation and social inadequacy.[1] It is significant that the definition adopted by the Commission made social competency the test of normality. According to this definition, "the feebleminded are persons who are capable of earning a living under favorable

[1] At the time most of the articles referred to in this chapter were written, the term, feebleminded, was used to designate those found to be below an assumed normal level of intelligence. It should be noted also, that according to British usage, the term "feebleminded," is the equivalent of the American terms high grade or mildly retarded.

circumstances, but are incapable from mental defect existing from birth or from an early age (a) of competing on equal terms with their normal fellows; or (b) of managing themselves and their affairs with ordinary prudence."

British Findings

The great amount of evidence which the Commission gathered was of a disturbing nature. This evidence revealed in striking manner the relation between retardation and various social ills. In dealing with the question of mental defect and crime, "the evidence points unmistakably to the fact that mentally defective children often have immoral tendencies; that they are greatly lacking in self-control; and moreover are peculiarly open to suggestion so that they are at the mercy of bad companions." [2] The medical officer of Pentonville Prison reported 40 percent of the juvenile offenders received in his institution as feebleminded.[3] The medical officer to the London County Council stated that if he could have fingerprints made of every child in the special classes, probably during the succeeding ten years a great number of them would be found under assumed names in maternity hospitals or in the hands of the police.

The testimony of prison medical officers generally estimated 20 percent of the prison population to be subnormal. It was especially noted that great numbers of habitual criminals were mentally deficient; one such person had been indicted 105 times previously. Besides the more serious offenses of murder, rape, arson, etc., there was found on every hand to be a great amount of begging, vagrancy, sleeping-out, and petty thieving. Ten percent of the tramps admitted to reformatories were shown to be deficient.

On the general question of subnormal criminals, the Commissioners had this to say: "Many competent observers are of the opinion that if the constantly recurring fatuous and irresponsible

[2] Abstract of British Royal Commission Report, pp. 6–7.
[3] Report of the British Royal Commission (1908), 8:23.

crimes and offenses of mentally defective persons are to be prevented, long and continuous detention is necessary."

It was no new finding that habitual inebriety was closely associated with retardation. Dr. Branthwaite, Inspector under the Inebriates Act, asserted: "Very many of these cases sent to us from courts are none other than just feebleminded persons, drunkards simply because they are feebleminded, their drunkenness being merely one evidence of their mental condition. . . . The women inebriates of this class, when out of control, go to swell the immoral classes." Of 771 cases admitted to the Brentry Reformatory, the Superintendent stated that only 30 percent were of fair mental capacity and capable, but for their drunken habits, of earning their own living.

SEXUAL IRREGULARITY The prevalence of sexual irregularities among the retarded was strikingly shown in the report of the Commission. The York Rescue Home reported 30 percent of those applying for admission as feebleminded—"many too bad to keep as they lower the standard of work too much and require such special treatment." A representative of the Church Penitentiary Association, said, "These cases of feeble minds and weak wills are a danger to the community. However carefully taught and trained during their two years' stay in a House of Mercy, they are sure to fall back into their old lives of sin from their inability to resist the temptation around them." The superintendent of the Royal Edinburgh Asylum, stated: "I have been devoting special attention to the previous history of the feebleminded who have been sent to the asylum as certified patients, especially the young women. . . . I have come to the conclusion that such persons in a large city are subject to overwhelming temptations and pressure toward sexual immorality. Many of them have had illegitimate children and this often at very early ages. . . . When illegitimate children are borne by such young women, the chances are enormously in favor of their turning out to be either imbeciles, or degenerates, or criminals."

The conclusions of the Commission were stated as follows: "We have pointed out how strong is the argument for the detention of the mentally defective in suitable institutions; and we have shown also that, except in cases in which the home fulfills the purpose, supervision and control should follow immediately on their leaving a special class or being found unsuitable for day school education."

Alarm in America

The report of the British Royal Commission coupled with work being done in the eugenics field was not long in arousing widespread concern about the problem of mental deficiency in this country. There began a series of studies, investigations, and reports. One of the earliest of these studies was made in New York City in 1910 by Dr. Anne Moore and published by the State Charities Aid Association. In the introduction, Dr. Moore stated: "My study of the situation in New York convinces me (1) that the horrors attendant upon feeblemindedness have in no way been exaggerated; (2) that the condition is neither circumscribed nor local; . . . (3) that there is a crying need for concerted action looking toward control of the situation." [4] In giving the consensus of opinion of the time on this subject, Dr. Moore stated that those who have studied the question "realize that the feebleminded are a menace to our present-day civilization and that the problem of caring for them can no longer with safety be ignored. They agree that the defect is often hereditary and incurable, that it leads to poverty, degeneracy, crime, and disease."

Under the leadership of Dr. Bernard Glueck, former Director of the Psychiatric Clinic, Sing Sing Prison, a study was made of about 600 consecutive admissions to Sing Sing during a period of nine months. As the fact was revealed that not less than 66.8 percent of the admissions studied had already served one or more previous terms in prisons or reformatories, the reasons for such a state of affairs were diligently sought. It became necessary to find a more scientific explanation than the one heretofore advanced, that such individuals were instinctive criminals or pre-

---

[4] Moore, *The Feebleminded in New York*, p. 11.

destined to lives of crime. Dr. Glueck found that no less than 59 percent of the 608 cases evinced, in addition to various conduct disorders, some form of nervous or mental abnormality, which had in some way affected their behavior. Twelve percent were mentally ill or deteriorated; 18.9 percent were classified as psychopathic; while 28.1 percent were intellectually defective. Recidivism was found in 80.6 percent of the intellectual defectives.[5]

PAUPERISM AND DEGENERACY   Alarm concerning the social consequences of mental retardation soon became country-wide. Along with the studies just considered, there was published during this period a great mass of material on the subject. This ranged from cautious, careful collections of information open, at the present time, merely to modification and shifting of emphasis, to the more hasty presentments which made of retardation a terrifying social specter. Practically all the writers, however, agreed that "feeblemindedness is the mother of crime, pauperism and degeneracy."

From his experience as medical director of the Municipal Court in Boston, Dr. V. V. Anderson wrote in 1917: "The feebleminded possibly form the most important single group of which our courts need to take cognizance. They furnish a substantial nucleus to that most expensive body of individuals who clog the machinery of justice, who spend their lives in and out of penal institutions and furnish data for the astonishing facts of recidivism." Dr. Anderson noted "a very well defined group . . . who fail to respond properly to any form of treatment, who on being released from prison very quickly find themselves again in court; who, when placed on probation, are usually surrendered, . . . who seem totally unable to adapt themselves to society's laws and customs, and thus are arrested over and over and over again. A study of this class indicates that feeblemindedness stands as a causative factor in from 25 percent to 40 percent of cases." [6]

[5] Glueck, "Concerning Prisoners," *Mental Hygiene*, 2:177–218.
[6] Anderson, "Feeblemindedness as Seen in Court," *Boston Medical and Surgical Journal*, 176:429–31.

In a pamphlet put out by the Department of Health and Charities, Philadelphia, entitled *The Degenerate Children of Feebleminded Women* is found the following: "Practically all poor, feebleminded women at large become the mothers of illegitimate children soon after reaching the age of puberty. . . . The histories of these feebleminded women and their feebleminded children are practically the same. Their unfortunate birth, helplessness, pauperism, and ruin is part of a continuous series whereby the community is constantly supplied with the elements of degeneracy."

Jean Weidensall in 1917 reported on an unselected series of unmarried mothers, from the obstetrical service of the Cincinnati General Hospital: "The results of the tests lead to the conclusion that not more than 20 percent of the unmarried mothers can be safely pronounced normal. . . . From 40 to 45 percent of the unmarried mothers are almost without question so low grade mentally as to make life under institutional care the only happy one for themselves and the most economical and the only safe arrangement for society." [7]

The Bureau of Juvenile Research of Ohio reported in 1915 mental examinations of 671 boys and 329 girls. By the Binet-Simon scale, 57 percent of these juveniles were found to be mentally deficient.

In a 1916 Public Health Report, W. L. Treadway observed: "The feebleminded are unable to follow regular employment and therefore add to the number of 'floating' or irregular employees. Owing to their tendency to become criminals and paupers, and to their inability to comprehend the principles of right living and personal hygiene, this group of individuals forms a large proportion of the penal population and adds materially to the spread of communicable diseases."

In 1912, Dr. Walter E. Fernald gave an address on the subject. To quote: "The social and economic burdens of uncomplicated feeblemindedness are only too well known. The feebleminded

---

[7] Weidensall, *Mentality of the Unmarried Mother*, National Conference of Social Work, Pittsburgh, 1917.

are a parasitic, predatory class, never capable of self-support or of managing their own affairs. The great majority ultimately become public charges in some form. They cause unutterable sorrow at home and are a menace and danger to the community. Feebleminded women are almost invariably immoral and . . . usually become carriers of venereal disease or give birth to children who are as defective as themselves. . . . Every feebleminded person, especially the high-grade imbecile, is a potential criminal, needing only the proper environment and opportunity for the development and expression of his criminal tendencies."

One could go on with such statements indefinitely so great was the bulk of material published on this side of the question. To give the consensus of these scattered opinions in the form of a summary of a fairly typical study: "Our data here reveal that illegitimacy, attempted murder, theft, forgery, arson, prostitution, drunkenness, destitution, and disease are salient features of the social careers of these incompetents."

Such was the social indictment. What the results were in terms of social action is shown in the following chapters.

VII. *Sterilization*

ASSUMING the validity of the foregoing evidence, a true indictment of mental deficiency as a social evil of tremendous proportions had been found. It had all taken place in an extremely short space of time as those things go. In 1900, with the exception of the small beginnings of the special class movement in the public schools, mental deficiency appeared almost entirely as an institutional problem and interest in it was confined for the most part to those directly concerned with custodial care. In the country at large, some 12,000 mental defectives, principally of the obvious type, were being cared for in state institutions. Judging by the number of cases under care and the public recognition it received (or rather failed to receive), mental deficiency in 1900 was an exceedingly small and insignificant social problem.

By 1915, mental deficiency had focused public attention as perhaps the largest and most serious social problem of the time. The many articles, pamphlets, and official reports which appeared, the many commissions, agencies, and committees which were organized to cope with the problem, were an evidence of this. There was widespread alarm. A number of states, among them New York, Pennsylvania, New Jersey, Massachusetts, Michigan, Indiana, Ohio, Kansas, Minnesota, and Virginia, appointed official investigating commissions to make a survey of the problem and recommend what action should be taken.

The principal concern was over the large number of mental defectives discovered to be at large in the community. As already noted, conservative estimates based on various surveys which preceded the findings of the army tests placed the number of mental defectives in the country at over 400,000. These estimates taken together with the current views on the biological and social implications of mental deficiency were rightly occasion for grave concern. There were some who suggested taking radical measures. The most extreme of these, which aimed at wiping out all mental deficiency at one fell blow, was that of euthanasia, putting the mentally deficient to death by some merciful means. The many reasons why this solution was not adopted or even seriously considered by responsible persons need scarcely be enumerated here. Attention centered upon two measures, either or both of which were considered desirable and practicable, i.e., sterilization and segregation.

At the meeting of the Research Committee of the Eugenics Section of the American Breeders' Association in May, 1911, a resolution was adopted appointing a committee to study and report on the best practical means of cutting off the defective germ-plasm in the American population.

Ten remedies suggested as possibly efficacious "for purging from the blood of the race the innately defective strains" were listed by the committee as follows:

1. Life segregation (or segregation during the reproductive period).
2. Sterilization.
3. Restrictive marriage laws and customs.
4. Eugenic education of the public and of prospective marriage mates.
5. Systems of matings purporting to remove defective traits.
6. General environmental betterment.
7. Polygamy.
8. Euthanasia.
9. Neo-Malthusianism.
10. Laissez-faire.

Of these the committee was of the opinion that the first two—life segregation and sterilization—held out the greatest hope of most immediate and effective results. As to the first, life segregation (or segregation during the reproductive period) it was stated: "This remedy must, in the opinion of the committee, be the principal agent used by society in cutting off its supply of defectives."

As to the second, sterilization, the committee reported: "Among the students of the eugenical status and movement of mankind there is a wide range of opinion as to the extremity to which society itself should go in applying sterilization, and concerning the part this remedy should play in relation to other remedial agencies. . . . In the program proposed by the committee sterilization is advocated only as supporting the more important feature of segregation when the latter agency fails to function eugenically. The relation between these two agencies is automatic, for it is proposed to sterilize only those individuals who, by due process of law, have been declared socially inadequate and have been committed to state custody, and are known to possess cacogenic potentialities. The committee has assumed that society must, at all hazards, protect its breeding stock, and it advocates sterilization only as supplementary to the segregation feature of the program, which is equally effective eugenically, and more effective socially."

Summarizing its findings, the committee stated: "Restrictive marriage laws and customs, eugenic education of the public, of prospective marriage consorts, and . . . of potential parents and general environmental betterment are all eugenic agencies of great value.

Statutes and Their Effect

Eugenic sterilization was adopted by a number of states in rapid succession. Indiana was the pioneer. Its sterilization measure became law on March 9, 1907. Washington, California, and Connecticut enacted similar statutes in 1909; New Jersey and Iowa followed in 1911, New York and Nevada in 1912. By 1926, twenty-three states had enacted such laws.[1]

[1] Laughlin, *Eugenical Sterilization* (New Haven, American Eugenics Society, 1926).

In the years that followed, new states joined the list and many already possessing sterilization statutes modified or amended existing laws. Indiana, the pioneer state in such legislation and temporarily absent from the group when its earlier statute had been declared unconstitutional, enacted a new law in 1927. North Dakota in 1927 enacted a new law to replace the one of 1913. In 1929 Delaware, Maine, Michigan, and Nebraska enacted strengthening amendments to their existing laws. On the other hand, after 1940 Washington dropped from the list and Alabama's law

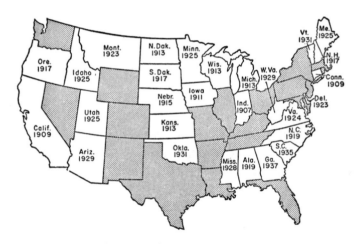

STATES HAVING STERILIZATION LAWS IN 1958

Date indicates the year in which a law was first passed; later revisions or amendments are not shown.

has not been used since 1935. But by 1955, twenty-eight states had sterilization laws on their statute books.

From the passage of the first sterilization law in 1907 to 1925, a period of eighteen years, a total of 6,244 eugenic operations were performed in the United States on all types of reputedly cacogenic persons, of which by far the largest number were on the mentally ill. On the mentally retarded a total of only 1,374 such operations had been performed, of which 64 percent were in one state, California. By 1942 there had been in all states 17,955 such operations on the subnormal, and by 1947 there had been 23,162. For this five-year period it will be seen that operations averaged about 1,000 a year throughout the country. California was again the most active. During 1954 only 571 operations were reported. By January, 1955, a total of 29,512 sterilization operations had been performed upon the mentally retarded, of which 7,503 were in California.

Therefore, it may be said that with the exception of California (and it should be pointed out here that the California program has been less active since 1951), eugenic sterilization as a measure of social control of the retarded has been little but a gesture. Even in California the number thus far sterilized is small compared with generally accepted estimates of the extent of mental retardation.

Moreover, states having sterilization laws vary widely in applying them. A number of factors enter. Probably the most decisive is the attitude of superintendents of institutions, some being greatly interested, others only moderately so. There are also great differences among institutions in the facilities available for performing operations. During World War II the absence of surgeons on military duty arbitrarily kept down the number of sterilizations. It must be remembered also that public opinion plays a great part, in some communities favoring sterilization, in others opposing it.

The courts of the nation have played no small role in influencing the effectiveness of sterilization statutes, and indeed, in allowing their very existence.

Curiously the sterilization law in New York seems to have been enacted without any organized public opinion back of it. It was passed without any action for or against it on the part of individuals and organizations in the state who would naturally have been interested in the measure. Nevertheless, the bill was passed in the Assembly with but few dissenting votes, in the Senate unanimously, and was promptly approved by the Governor.

But in its operation the New York law was a complete fiasco and is a telling instance of how little any law can accomplish

TABLE I. STERILIZATIONS OF THE MENTALLY DEFICIENT REPORTED IN THE
U.S. TO JANUARY 1, 1958

Cumulative Totals [a]

State	Total	Male	Female
Alabama [b]	224	129	95
Arizona	6		6
California	7,518	3,417	4,101
Connecticut	130	25	105
Delaware	575	244	331
Georgia	630	240	390
Idaho	20	6	14
Indiana	1,728	852	876
Iowa	828	189	639
Kansas	849	511	338
Maine	219	39	180
Michigan	2,864	811	2,053
Minnesota	1,910	396	1,514
Mississippi	58	14	44
Montana	214	55	159
Nebraska	684	337	347
New Hampshire	379	125	254
New York [b]			
North Carolina	3,102	526	2,576
North Dakota	560	218	342
Oklahoma	250	51	199
Oregon	1,252	456	796
South Carolina	131	12	119
South Dakota	742	268	474
Utah	632	296	336
Vermont	211	73	138
Virginia	3,205	1,272	1,933
Washington [b]	276	33	243
West Virginia	52	11	41
Wisconsin	1,789	384	1,405
Totals	31,038	10,990	20,048

[a] Number of sterilizations performed since each state law was enacted. For length of time, see map.
 [b] Not reported:
 Alabama: enacted law in 1919; still on books, has been inoperative since 1935 when state supreme court rendered an adverse opinion regarding broader sterilization legislation then pending.

New York: enacted law in 1912; declared unconstitutional in 1918 on
the ground it denied equal protection of the law because of not including
those outside as well as inside institutions.
Washington: enacted law in 1909; declared unconstitutional in 1942 because of technical deficiencies in the act.

without public opinion behind it. Thirty state institutions were
subject to the act. Operations upon 41 female patients in state
hospitals and upon one male inmate of the State Prison at Auburn
were performed under its authority. But not a single inmate of a
state school was sterilized. In 1915, in a test case, proceedings
were initiated in the Supreme Court of Albany County for the
purpose of securing authority to sterilize one of the male patients
in the Rome State School for Mental Defectives. The Court held
the statute "unconstitutional and invalid" on the ground of class
legislation, and perpetually enjoined the performance of such an
operation. In his opinion, Mr. Justice Rudd stated: "The provisions of the Federal Constitution to which this law is offensive
is that part of the Fourteenth Amendment which declares that
'no state . . . shall deny to any person within its jurisdiction the
equal protection of the laws.' " The judgment was unanimously
affirmed by the Appellate Division in 1918. While an appeal was
pending before the Court of Appeals, the statute was repealed by
the legislature in 1920.

In 1926, Dr. H. H. Laughlin of the former Eugenics Record
Office reported on the status of sterilization legislation in the
twenty-three states which up to that time had passed such laws.
He found these laws functioning satisfactorily in only four of the
twenty-three states, California, Kansas, Nebraska, and Oregon.
In none of these four states, however, had the laws been tested in
the courts. In four states, Indiana, Nevada, New Jersey, and New
York, the laws had been declared unconstitutional and were, of
course, inoperative. In eight states where the laws were regarded
as functioning only moderately well (a comparatively small number of operations having been performed), Connecticut, Delaware, Idaho, Iowa, Michigan, New Hampshire, North Dakota,
and Virginia, the laws had been tested in the courts of only two
of these—Michigan and Virginia—but in both the statutes had

been declared constitutional by the State Supreme Court, and in the case of Virginia, by the Supreme Court of the United States. Of the seven remaining states, five had enacted legislation too recently before the publication of Dr. Laughlin's report for experience in those states to warrant judgment as to the significance of their laws, and in two of them, the laws, while still on the statute books, were dead letters.

In some of the earlier sterilization statutes, the punitive motive was prominent, and sterilization was made the penalty for certain sexual crimes. These laws were, for the most part, declared unconstitutional on the grounds that such use of sterilization constituted "cruel and unusual punishment." In these earlier statutes also, the therapeutic motive sometimes appeared, that is, sterilization was authorized with the object of improving the physical and mental condition of the individual. But, as Dr. Laughlin pointed out, sterilization for this purpose is without point, as existing laws relating to surgical practice permit operations upon the reproductive organs when indicated as necessary for the physical well-being of the individual.

Consequently, in modern sterilization legislation, the objective has been wholly eugenic, that is, to decrease the number of defectives in the next generation. The model sterilization law drafted by Dr. Laughlin in the light of past experience and court decisions and published by the American Eugenics Society states that the purpose of the law is "to prevent the procreation of persons socially inadequate from defective inheritance." Subsequent sterilization laws, such as that of Virginia, have substantially followed this statute.

COURT DECISIONS   We have already seen that a number of state laws were declared unconstitutional by the courts in test cases. Therefore, the decision of the United States Supreme Court handed down in 1927 upholding the Virginia sterilization statute had great significance and gave impetus not only to the passage of additional sterilization laws but also to their enforcement once they were on the statute books.

Virginia's sterilization law was enacted in 1924 and has since been only slightly modified. The object of the law, stated in its preamble, is frankly eugenic and is based on the premise that heredity plays an important part in the genesis of mental disease, mental retardation, epilepsy, and crime. The law applies to inmates of the state institutions for mental defectives, epileptics, and the mentally ill, and specifically states that the operation if upon a male shall be vasectomy, and if upon a female, salpingectomy.

It provides that the superintendent of the institution, before proceeding with the sterilization operation on any patient, shall first present a petition to the special board of directors of his institution, asking the board for an order requiring him to carry out the operation. A copy of this petition must be served upon the patient and also upon the legal guardian or committee of the patient. The special board is required to consider evidence on the petition, and it is specifically provided that the patient may, if desired, appear in person at the hearing. Any party to the proceedings has the right to be represented by counsel.

If the special board grants the order, the operation may be performed in not less than thirty days from the date of such order, unless within that time an appeal of right is taken to the Circuit Court of the county or city in which the institution is located. Provision is also made for appeal within ninety days after the final order of the Circuit Court to the Supreme Court of Appeals of the state. A special paragraph provides: "Neither any of said superintendents nor any other person legally participating in the execution of the provisions of this act shall be liable either civilly or criminally on account of said participation."

In the first test case, that of a woman, a mentally deficient patient of the State Colony for Epileptics and Feebleminded in Virginia, an order directing the operation of salpingectomy was issued by the special board of directors of the Colony. The Circuit Court of Amherst County sustained the decision of the board, and in 1925, the Supreme Court of Appeals of Virginia, in affirming the decision of the Circuit Court, declared the law a valid enactment under state and Federal constitutions.

The opinion of the United States Supreme Court on the Virginia statute as delivered by Mr. Justice Holmes on May 2, 1927, stated in part: "We have seen more than once that the public welfare may call upon the best citizens for their lives. It would be strange if it could not call upon those who already sap the strength of the State for these lesser sacrifices, often not felt to be such by those concerned, in order to prevent our being swamped with incompetents. It is better for all the world, if instead of waiting to execute degenerate offspring for crime, or to let them starve for their imbecility, society can prevent those who are manifestly unfit from continuing their kind. The principle that sustains compulsory vaccination is broad enough to cover the cutting of the Fallopian tubes. . . . Three generations of imbeciles are enough."

Sterilization legislation successfully met the challenge of constitutionality. But the problem of retardation is more a social one than a legal one. Does such legislation reduce the number of mental defectives? And what becomes of the patients who undergo such operations?

CALIFORNIA FINDINGS   A study of California's experience with eugenic sterilization was undertaken in 1926 under the general direction of E. S. Gosney, a philanthropist of Pasadena. Paul Popenoe, well known as a proponent of eugenics and as a writer in this field, was engaged to carry out this study with the assistance of an advisory council.[2]

The portion of Popenoe's study relating to the retarded includes the records of 605 patients (mostly between fifteen and twenty-five years of age, with a mean I.Q. of 60) representing practically all of the patients sterilized while residents of the Sonoma State Home, who were then out in the community. The mean time since parole from the institution was twenty months

[2] Popenoe, "Success on Parole after Sterilization," *Journal of Psycho-Aesthenics*, 32:86–103.

for both sexes, with a distribution range of from a few weeks to ten years or more.

In tabulating the results of his inquiries into the success of these sterilized patients in the community, Mr. Popenoe furnished information on 411 of the 605, or about 68 percent of the group, leaving 32 percent in the categories of unknown or omitted. The outcome of the 411 cases showed a considerably larger number of successes than failures, both among the males and females. Of the 107 males in the group of 411, 78 were regarded as successful, 28 as unsuccessful, and only one as doubtful. Of the 304 females, 189 were regarded as successful, 97 as unsuccessful, and 18 as doubtful.

To consolidate the results still further, Popenoe arbitrarily divided the doubtful cases equally between the successful and the unsuccessful, and classified the group as follows: Males—successful, 72.89 percent, unsuccessful 27.11 percent; females—successful, 65.35 percent, unsuccessful, 34.65 percent.

Popenoe interpreted success on parole as meaning that the individual was well-behaved, self-supporting (or supported from a legitimate source), apparently happy, and that the interests of society were as well protected as if the individual had remained at the institution. Accepting his interpretation, the behavior of these paroled groups compared favorably with the behavior of groups paroled from other institutions.

Popenoe made a special endeavor to answer the question in which students of sterilization are particularly interested, namely, that of sex behavior. His findings with regard to boys led him to conclude that "in none of the failures (save the doubtful case of the exhibitionist) was there any sexual element, and none of them gave evidence of being likely to become a focus for the dissemination of venereal diseases."

Prior to commitment, none of the males in this series had ever been married or been an illegitimate father. Less than one-fifth had shown tendencies that might possibly have resulted in reproduction, and as Popenoe recognized, many of these would not have reached an adult level of sexual behavior. Only 1½ percent of the sterilized boys had married after the operation and release from the institution. As Popenoe stated: "The conclusion must be that the feebleminded male of the class committed to the Sonoma State Home who would ever become a parent is exceptional." [3]

Such facts would seem to indicate that sterilization of males is to little purpose. To sterilize 100 percent of the males released from the institution in order to prevent procreation on the part of perhaps not more than 2 or 3 percent, appears a rather unnecessary procedure. Segregation, followed by well-organized supervision of the few showing heterosexual trends (which supervision is necessary for other than eugenic reasons) would seem to be the simpler and more direct method of dealing with this problem so far as males are concerned.

With females, the situation is, of course, different. Three-fourths of the girls and women admitted to Sonoma had previous records of sex delinquency, and in this group, 76 of the females had had a total of 223 pregnancies, not all illegitimate. When selected women of this type are returned to the community following a period of institutional training, sterilization is a means of preventing a certain number of children being born to them either within or without wedlock.

One of the dangers believed to be inherent in sterilization was that freedom from fear of pregnancy would encourage sterilized women to promiscuity and would result in an increased spread of venereal diseases. Popenoe's study gave no support to this belief. Among the 304 sterilized mentally retarded females returned to the community, he found only 25, or 8 percent, in whom sexual delinquency was marked. He concluded "that it is possible to parole a large number of sterilized girls or boys and to get a percentage of successes among them that compares favorably with any series of unsterilized cases of equal size that we have found elsewhere."

The findings of Popenoe's study were confirmed by a second

[3] Popenoe, "Fecundity of the Feebleminded," Eugenic Sterilization in California (unpublished).

independent survey conducted by him and E. S. Gosney that covered a twenty-eight-year period ending in 1938. One section, concerning 966 paroled sterilized girls, indicated that only 21, or about 2 percent, were maladjusted to the extent that they were a menace in the community. The report stated: "Among 425 feebleminded girls committed to California institutions, 9 out of every 12 had been sex delinquents. After commitment, sterilization and return to the community on parole, only 1 out of every 12 was a sex delinquent."

A study made by Dr. Fred O. Butler confirms further the findings of the earlier surveys.[4] This study covered the twenty-five-year period between 1919 and 1943. During that time 4,310 patients of the Sonoma State Home, of which Dr. Butler was then superintendent, were sterilized. During the same period 4,135 were discharged, and of this number 2,169, or 52.4 percent, had been sterilized. To the question, "Does sterilization tend to increase promiscuity, venereal disease, and sex delinquency?", Dr. Butler answered definitely, "No."

SCIENTIFIC ASPECTS Although the Supreme Court decision of 1927 established the constitutional soundness of legislation authorizing eugenic sterilization, there are today many authorities who do not accept as established the premises, biological, medical and social, which such legislation assumes. The social values of eugenic sterilization and the justification therefor are matters of divided opinion among scientists. There has also been much popular and religious opposition to sterilization as an undue invasion of personal rights.

The chief reasons advanced for sterilization by its proponents may be summed up as follows:

1. Sterilization, while no longer regarded as a panacea for mental retardation, will nevertheless reduce the number of defectives in the next generation to a very appreciable extent, and to that extent reduce the burdens which their presence in society entails.

[4] Butler, "Sterilization Procedure and Its Success in California." Reprint of National Conference of Juvenile Agencies, Jackson, Miss., 1925.

2. Sterilization must supplement segregation as a measure of control to prevent procreation because (a) no state has sufficient institutional facilities for all the subnormal; (b) insofar as it can be substituted for segregation, sterilization relieves the state of a heavy financial burden; (c) in practice, many high grade cases are paroled or discharged each year from state institutions, and in such cases sterilization is a wise precautionary measure.

3. Marriage, which often offers an opportunity of socially stabilizing the higher grade girls, can be regarded as a satisfactory adjustment if the girl is sterilized, but cannot be so regarded if she is able to have children.

4. Aside from all eugenic considerations, mental defectives should be denied parenthood because not intellectually equipped to give the proper training and environment to their children.

Opponents of sterilization have based their attitude on a consideration of several questions which it seems to them have not been satisfactorily answered. Logically, the first concerns the hereditary character of mental deficiency. The assumption on which eugenic sterilization is based—that mental deficiency is preponderantly hereditary according to certain well-known laws, is an assumption that is not supported by recent research as will be seen in Chapter X. Therefore, the question: Why adopt so drastic a measure as sterilization, supposedly to control an hereditary process, the extent and mechanism of which are far from being clear?

Even if the hereditary assumption were granted, a second question is, how effective would sterilization be in reducing the number of mental defectives in subsequent generations in view of the fact that large numbers of normal persons carry faulty genes and that thousands of mental defectives outside of institutions will remain unsterilized? Dr. A. F. Tredgold, leading English authority on mental deficiency, personally held that the offspring of mental defectives are almost invariably subnormal, and often actually defective. Nevertheless, he asserted that "As a matter of fact, my own observations show that, in relation to the total number of defectives, the proportion of those who are the offspring of a certifiably defective parent, or parents, is extremely small. . . .

It follows that if every defective in existence a generation ago had been sterilized, the number of defectives today would not have been appreciably diminished. It also follows that if every defective now existing were to be sterilized, the result a generation hence would be insignificant. In short, in order to produce any marked decrease in the total number of mental defectives a generation hence, it would be necessary to sterilize, or otherwise prevent the propagation of, not merely those who are themselves defectives, but all those who are 'carriers'; that is to say, every person suffering from germ vitiation. Obviously, this is not merely impracticable, but it is impossible. . . . We are compelled to conclude, therefore, that from the point of view of prevention, sterilization would not do what is claimed for it and that its results would be relatively slight." [5]

In keeping with this view were the results of a study made in 1926 by the Mental Deficiency Committee of the Surrey (England) County Council. This was an analysis of family histories of 500 consecutive cases of mental defectives coming to public attention in that county. To quote the report: "In 25 percent only of such cases was one parent in any way abnormal mentally, and in four cases only, i.e., 0.08 percent, were both parents defective (and some of these might not be certifiable under the Act). Further, in the same families, some of the children were apparently normal. It would appear that if every defective now existing were to be sterilized, the result a generation hence, would be insignificant."

A third unanswered question is, to what extent does the mere prevention of procreation avail if the behavior of the individual remains unaffected? Sterilization in itself cannot be expected to increase the sense of social responsibility. The mental defective who was not safe to be at large before sterilization will be no safer merely because of sterilization. Social danger lies in the fact that once sterilization is accomplished, the temptation is to release the individual from institutional care without special training or fitness for community life. For as long as the individual

[5] Tredgold, "The Sterilization of Mental Defectives," *Mental Welfare,* 7:35-41.

is institutionalized, sterilization is superfluous. Segregation accomplishes all that sterilization does in preventing propagation, but does even more in protecting the individual from social failure.

Still another question concerns itself with the practical difficulty placed upon those who have the serious responsibility of administering a sterilization statute, of deciding in individual instances whether a particular person should properly be deprived of procreative powers. The conscientious official would first wish to be sure that the person in question is truly mentally deficient. But sterilization is not primarily directed at the obvious, low-grade cases, who, because of a lack of sex attraction, or potency, or both, are not so likely to propagate. It is the higher-grade cases, who are physically more attractive, and who frequently pass for normal, at whom sterilization legislation is mainly directed. It is generally agreed that when one is dealing with borderline intelligence levels, one cannot safely generalize and that the intelligence quotient alone is not a safe guide. If an undoubted diagnosis can be made, a greater difficulty arises in deciding whether, in the particular instance, the defect is of an hereditary character. Certainly, there is no warrant for depriving an individual of the ability to have offspring unless these points can be determined to the entire satisfaction of the administrative officials.

To the author, who has endeavored to weigh available evidence and opinions on all sides of the question, sterilization fails to recommend itself, in the present state of our knowledge, as a measure of social control to be generally applied to the subnormal. From the point of view of succeeding generations, it appears doubtful that sterilization would reduce the number of mental defectives sufficiently to be of any general social significance, or to have any appreciable effect on public expenditures. From the point of view of the present generation, sterilization can in no sense be a substitute for constructive training and community programs reenforced by research and treatment.

VIII. *Segregation*

WHILE there was from the first much disagreement on the subject of sterilization, there was a very general agreement in favor of segregation as the most practicable and acceptable means of care.

About 1910, the prevalent alarm concerning retardation resulted in many states in the appointment of special investigating commissions, and in vigorous and well-organized campaigns of publicity and legislative activity directed toward the provision of institutional facilities sufficient to segregate all mental defectives. A brief résumé of what was said and done in New York in connection with this campaign is given as typical of the experience of many other states.

In 1910, the Public Education Association of New York began a study, under the direction of Dr. Anne Moore, of the status of retarded children who had gone out from the New York City public schools. Dr. Moore, after citing numerous cases to show how serious a social problem the mentally deficient created, emphasized that the only way to deal effectively with this problem "is to provide supervision and care that will last during the whole lifetime of the feebleminded individual, certainly during the reproductive period."

The publication of this report was the means of stimulating the first extensive public interest in New York State in the care of the mentally deficient. An immediate result was the appointment by the State Charities Aid Association of a special Committee on Provision for the Feebleminded which was organized to carry on an educational campaign and to secure more adequate institutional care for the mentally defective. The Association from year to year brought the situation forcefully to the attention of the legislature. Careful studies of the mental deficiency problem were made, and appeals to the legislature were based upon concrete evidence.

In 1914, as a result of the manifest public concern about the problem, the New York legislature created a "State Commission to Investigate Provision for the Mentally Deficient." This Commission, which reported in 1915, obtained the testimony of a large number of persons relating directly or indirectly to the problem of mental deficiency in New York and other states. The report of this Commission verified the inadequacy of the existing state institutions for the retarded. These institutions, it pointed out, then provided for not more than 3,000, whereas the Commission had definitely learned of 21,000 known mental defectives in the state who were outside of institutions and who needed or were likely to need institutional care. "The mentally defective man or woman at liberty," the report states, "constitutes a serious menace to the State. In many cases, the mental defect is hereditary and is liable to be transmitted . . . to succeeding generations. This danger is in turn aggravated by the well-known propagating tendency of the feebleminded, and because they are in most cases potential delinquents or criminals, peculiarly susceptible to the suggestions of evil-minded associates. There is, therefore, urgent need for a large extension of the present facilities of the State institutions." This Commission also strongly urged separate institutions for the confirmed male and female defective delinquents where such habitual social offenders might have indefinite custodial care.

Notwithstanding the determined efforts of organizations and individuals, of official boards and commissions, the segregation program in New York failed to make progress at all commensurate with the demand. In 1910, the New York State institutions, together with the New York City institution on Randall's Island, provided accommodations for 3,636 patients. In the decade 1910–1920, no new institution was created, although Letchworth Village, at Thiells, Rockland County, established in 1907, was first opened for the reception of patients in 1911. Appropriations were dealt out, moreover, on such a meager scale from year to year for the development of Letchworth Village, that by 1920 it provided accommodations for only 811 patients. On July 1, 1920, the four state schools, Newark, Rome, Syracuse, and Letchworth Village, together with Randall's Island, had a total bed capacity (exclusive of beds in colonies) of 5,296, or 51 per 100,000 population, as compared with 3,636 beds, or 40 per 100,000 population in 1910.

Thus, in spite of the growing alarms regarding deficiency, and the concentration of effort on the part of all concerned toward rapid enlargement of institutional facilities, the segregation program did not make substantial headway in view of the then reputed size of the problem. In other words, the provision in ten years' time of 1,660 additional beds, after the expenditure of so much effort, seemed small as compared with the new estimate of 40,000 retarded persons in the state who were outside of institutions, especially when it is kept in mind that the aim of the segregation program was to segregate *all* mental defectives during their lifetime, or at least during the reproductive period. World War I may perhaps be blamed for the failure of state authorities to provide more liberally for new construction. There is no doubt that war conditions did result in a reduction of legislative appropriations for such purposes, but even if the rate of appropriations of the years before and after the war for new construction had been maintained during the war years, the result for the decade would not have been very much greater.

The history of Letchworth Village is illuminating in this connection. In the thirty-one years from the opening of the Rome institution in 1894, to the authorization of the institution at Wassaic in 1925, the only new institutional project for the retarded that New York attempted was Letchworth Village. Officially authorized in 1907, it might have been expected that Letchworth Village would have been pushed rapidly to completion under the impetus of the alarmist urge. The plans called for an institution of at least 3,000 beds. That goal was reached only after twenty years of effort and waiting. The special $50,000,000 bond issue of 1923 made $2,987,000 available for this purpose and hastened development.

The practical impossibility, under the greatest pressure, of obtaining from the legislature, and ultimately the taxpayers, appropriations sufficient to provide anything like complete segregation led to the development of a program of much more modest scope. Indeed, as the problem has been further studied, it is now believed that only a small fraction of the mentally deficient need institutional care.

The first movement of national scope to undertake organized effort in behalf of more effective state laws and increased institutional provision for the retarded was the Committee on Provision for the Feebleminded formed in 1914. This Committee had its origin a year previous as the Extension Department of the institution at Vineland, and was inspired by Dr. E. R. Johnstone and Dr. H. H. Goddard of that institution. Its aim was to carry the Vineland message of the need for inclusive care and control of the mentally retarded to other parts of the country. Alexander Johnson was the Field Secretary of this Committee, and upon him fell the active work, which consisted largely of public lectures and appearances before legislative bodies. About 1,100 lectures were given in 33 states before an aggregate of 250,000 people. The Committee carried on this national program for about three years, when it relinquished the field to the National Committee for Mental Hygiene, which, in the meantime, had organized a Division on Mental Deficiency. The efforts made by the Committee led to the establishment of state institutions in nine states where no such provision had previously existed, the establishment of one or more additional institutions in five states already having at least one institution for this class, substantial additions to existing institutions in four other states.

This national effort for increasing institutional facilities, aided by the work of the National Committee for Mental Hygiene, state welfare organizations, special committees and other national groups, had the same general result as the effort in New York. In 1904, before the beginning of general public agitation, the number of patients in institutions for the retarded was 14,347, or 17.5 per 100,000 population. In 1910, the number of institutional patients had increased to 20,731 or 22.5 per 100,000 population. In the 13 years from 1910 to 1923 (during which time the most active propaganda for increased institutional accommodations was carried on) the number of patients provided for in institutions rose to 42,954 or 39.3 per 100,000 population. Data from the National Institute of Mental Health show that in 1956 with 107,382 resident patients, the national rate was 66.1 per 100,000 population. The rate varied from state to state. The median was 83.9, the low 8.1, and the high 163.7 per 100,000 population.[1] These figures plainly reveal that the objective of complete segregation did not even approximate realization. If we estimate the number of retarded persons in the country as a whole on the usual basis, the institutional accommodations of 1923 cared for less than 2 percent of the problem. In February, 1957, the average cost of care in an institution was about $1,100 a year. In a very few states patients are accepted without charge, but most institutions expect parents, if able, to pay for care according to their means. The charges are sometimes very substantial.

It is a matter of history that the two principal measures of social control on which main reliance was placed, during this period of alarm, for coping with the problem of mental deficiency, namely, sterilization and segregation, failed to meet the situation as completely as the proponents of these measures had expected. Viewing the problem as a whole, these measures touched only a relatively small part of it. It therefore became a practical necessity for those charged with official responsibility for the care of mental defectives to develop ways and means of dealing with them in the community. It is with these extra-institutional measures that the later chapters of this volume particularly deal.

[1] The National Institute of Mental Health publishes a yearly bulletin showing the number of mental defectives in institutions.

There can be no doubt that institutional provision is basic to any modern program for the care and training of mental defectives. The present conception of the role of the institution, however, is different from what it was. In modern programs institutional care is frankly not intended for all, or even a majority of mental defectives. The institution receives selected cases particularly needing that type of care. Nevertheless, the development of community programs for the training and supervision of mental defectives, far from diminishing the demands upon the institution, has actually increased the need for institutional facilities. These community programs serve to discover previously unknown cases for whom institutional provision is especially desirable. Therefore, the institution remains today a most important and indispensable factor in the care of the mentally deficient.

IX. *Defective Delinquents*

A most troublesome class of mental defectives for whom special measures of control have long been needed are the so-called "defective delinquents." The term is applied to those in whom antisocial tendencies are found to be so deep-seated as to require care and treatment quite different from that of the usual mental deficiency institution. Life-long custody of many of this class may be desirable. Defective delinquents have been found to constitute but a small minority of the mentally deficient; yet they have proved vastly more troublesome in the community and in institutions for mental deficiency than all of the rest.

In any large group of offenders, there is usually to be found a certain proportion of defective delinquents. Unless custody for an indeterminate period and, if necessary, for life is provided for this class, they appear with regularity before the courts as recidivists, and constitute a heavy burden upon society. It is of this relatively small group that many of the assertions as to antisocial behavior, made in the social indictment previously described, are substantially true.

The institutional custody and training of this class of mentally deficient offenders presents a distinct problem. For those who have actually been convicted of offenses, the usual penal procedures of probation, determinate sentence, and parole, on the assumption that the offender has normal potentialities and can be socially rehabilitated, do not successfully apply. For the others, the younger group for the most part, who have committed no serious overt acts, but whose antisocial tendencies are recognized, and who are committed to the regular state schools for mental defectives, the usual training methods also fall short.

Dr. Fernald and others have borne witness to the serious difficulties which the presence of even a small number of such defective delinquents in the ordinary institution creates. Dr. Fernald described the defective delinquent type as seen in his institution:

Many of this class are defiant, abusive, profane, disobedient, destructive, and incorrigible generally. They honestly feel that they are unjustly confined. . . . They frequently attack those who are responsible for their custody. They resent any effort to amuse or entertain them. They cannot be discharged because they are not safe persons for community life. . . . It is most unfortunate that this criminal type of defective . . . should complicate the care and training of the ordinary defective . . . who constitutes the legitimate problem of a school for feebleminded.[1]

Another superintendent compared the difficulties of housing defective delinquents with average patients, to introducing gangsters into a kindergarten. A few of these difficult ones can terrorize a whole ward, disrupt routine, and exhaust the staff. State schools are not organized for dealing with this type, being planned for large numbers of relatively mild defectives, more amenable to socialization.

Some Special Programs

MASSACHUSETTS Recognizing the urgency of this problem, a number of states have made special institutional provision for defective delinquents. As early as 1910, Dr. Fernald formulated for Massachusetts the first law in this country providing for the separate segregation of defective delinquents. This law was passed in 1911. It was designed to relieve the state schools of the disproportionate burden of their most incorrigible and disturbing elements and to remove defectives from the prisons by providing a special place for the custody of this type. The law also provided for commitments directly from the courts, and further that all commitments should be for an indeterminate period.

[1] Annual Report, Massachusetts State School for the Feebleminded, Waltham, 1921.

It took eleven years actually to bring that law into effect. Finally in 1922 a division for male defective delinquents was opened at the Massachusetts State Farm at Bridgewater, followed in 1926 by a division at the same place for female defective delinquents. In 1941 a department for a selected group was opened at the Reformatory for Women. In 1942, because of overcrowding at the State Farm, a number of men were transferred to the Massachusetts Reformatory for Men. This brought to four the departments for defective delinquents maintained by Massachusetts.

During the legislative session of 1928, the Massachusetts law was amended to include what is regarded as a satisfactory working definition of defective delinquency. As amended in 1952 it reads in part as follows:

If a person is found to be mentally defective. . . . If, after a hearing and examination of the person's record, character and personality, the court finds that such person has shown himself to be dangerous or shown a tendency to becoming such, that such tendency is or may become a menace to the public and that such person is not a proper subject for the schools for the feebleminded or commitment as an insane person, the court shall make a report of the finding to the effect that the person is a defective delinquent and may commit him to a department for defective delinquents according to his age and sex, as hereinafter provided.

A clear definition is an obvious aid to judges in distinguishing more carefully than they have done in the past the defective delinquent type.

Although under the Commissioner of Correction, the Massachusetts Division at Bridgewater has little of the prison flavor. Discipline is necessarily more rigid than in the ordinary mental deficiency institution, but emphasis is placed on treatment rather than on punishment. There are no cells. Inmates are housed in separate rooms with outside windows. Organized medical work, educational work, recreation and industrial training are provided. The care given, once chiefly custodial, has developed through the years to rehabilitation of the whole personality, with possible return to the community as a goal. At the discretion of the officials in charge inmates may be recommended for parole.

The complete separation of the defective delinquents in Massachusetts was a boon to the superintendents of the mental deficiency institutions. When the male division at Bridgewater was first opened, Dr. George Wallace, then Superintendent of the Wrentham State School, transferred 33 of the 1,400 cases in his institution. Among these 33 was a group of boys who had been guilty of acts of arson about the institution, as well as other offenses of a serious nature. Dr. Wallace stated that these 33 had caused more difficulty in the institution than all of the rest put together. Relieved of this burden, the institution was able to go forward with its training program for the other patients with much greater efficiency.

Dr. Fernald gave testimony to the same effect. He described the critical situation which existed in his institution the year before the Bridgewater division for male delinquents was opened. During this year a small group of defective delinquents had banded together in rebellion against the institutional discipline and had so injured five employes that these employes refused to continue in service. Escapes became a matter of daily occurrence and the demoralizing example of this small group was permeating the whole institution. Dr. Fernald had this to say about the effect on his own institution of the transfer of this small group:

The commitment of these 15 defective delinquents . . . had a most miraculous effect upon the morale and discipline of the school; in fact, overnight, the boys remaining in that department became courteous, obedient and willingly . . . went to work. There has not been a trace of any disciplinary trouble with them from that time. In fact, the whole group of male patients has been most favorably affected by the removal of this criminal group.[2]

On the other hand, under the more rigid discipline of the Bridgewater division, where the program could be specially

[2] Annual Report, Massachusetts State School for the Feebleminded, 1922, p. 19.

directed to this type of defective, this formerly unruly group was reported as giving practically no trouble. All of which reveals the advantages of classification and specialization in institutional work.

A word may be said about the favorable effect of removing defective delinquents from prisons, where they are misfits in a different way. They are looked down upon, often persecuted, by the more intelligent inmates and sometimes require segregation for their own protection. The prison training program is designed for those of average ability, and defectives profit little from it.

NEW YORK   In New York a department for female defective delinquents was established by law in 1920 at the Bedford Reformatory for Women and opened shortly thereafter. In 1931 the Albion State Training School (formerly Western House of Refuge) assumed care of defective delinquent women. The law governing this institution is similar to that for the New York institution for male defective delinquents described below.

By act of legislature in 1921, New York established a special state institution for male defective delinquents at Napanoch. This institution was opened on June 1, 1921. It took over the existing plant of the former Eastern New York Reformatory. Although Massachusetts had the first statute providing for such an institution, New York's Napanoch became the first separate institution in actual operation in this country for defective delinquents.

The law relating to the Napanoch institution provides that it is for the care, training and custody of male mental defectives over sixteen years of age, charged with, arraigned for, or convicted of criminal offenses. Napanoch may receive cases from the state schools for mental defectives who have committed more or less serious offenses while in the institution or before admission there, provided they have reached the age of sixteen or over; it may also receive by transfer from the prisons and reformatories those serving sentences (other than for murder in the first degree) who, upon examination, are found to be mentally defective; and, in addition, it may receive cases committed directly to it by the courts. The great majority in the institution are court commitments.

Napanoch originally had a capacity of 496 inmates. It was soon more than filled and the capacity has since been greatly increased. In the beginning, it was populated largely by transfers from the prisons, with a small proportion of transfers from state schools for mental defectives.[3] The courts were at first rather slow to use this new institution. Later, however, as the courts came to use the institution more and more, it received all of its new cases either from the courts or by transfer from penal institutions.

A distinctive feature of all commitments to Napanoch is that by law they are for life, if in the judgment of the superintendent of the institution the inmate's release to society is not warranted. In those cases which have been given definite prison sentences, the superintendent may not parole or discharge them before they would have been paroled or discharged if they had remained in a regular penal institution; nevertheless, such cases may be retained indefinitely beyond expiration of sentence by court order made upon the recommendation of the superintendent of the institution. All cases transferred from state institutions for mental defectives, or committed directly by the courts, may likewise be retained for life. Thus the state by law has recognized the existence of a class of persons whose defects are such that they may never be safely returned to the community, and has given its sanction to lifelong custody of such individuals. In this way, the problem of recidivism has been somewhat reduced. Likewise, the state institutions for mental defectives and the state prisons and reformatories have been, to some extent, relieved of a class of cases with which they are not well equipped to deal. The Woodbourne Correctional Institution was opened in 1935 and by 1950 had a certified capacity of 750. It admitted both defective delinquents and normal male delinquents by transfer. Since the latter part of 1950 it has not received mental de-

[3] Before the institution was placed under the Department of Correction.

fectives, all of whom have been transferred to Napanoch. Wood-bourne now admits borderline and dull normal inmates by transfer from institutions under the Department of Correction.

Napanoch has been conducted both along the lines of a penal institution and of a mental deficiency institution. Many of the high-grade type with strong criminal proclivities have been regarded as needing treatment primarily of a correctional and, at times, disciplinary character. The housing facilities include cell-blocks. For the inmates received from the state prisons, and to a large degree from the courts, this type of custody has been considered advisable. For others, dormitory provision of the usual institution type has been made. For the first six years of its existence, the Napanoch institution was administered under the direction of the State Commission for Mental Defectives, but following the reorganization of the New York state government, it was assigned to the jurisdiction of the State Department of Correction.

A special study of over 500 cases in the Napanoch institution showed the median mental age of the group by the Terman Revision to be 9.19 years, and by the Pintner-Patterson tests, 9.3 years. Nearly 80 percent were borderline or high-grade types. The psychiatric study of the same group showed 85 percent to have the characteristic reactions of psychopathic personality with problems in childhood, characterized by stubbornness, irritability, insubordination, truancy, etc. Many had records of lying and petty thievery. In the institution, the same type of personality was revealed in selfishness, untruthfulness, unreliability, instability, lack of sentiment, and lack of honor with fellow inmates. Over 60 percent of the group were classified as habitual offenders, having been arrested and placed on probation or committed to an institution at least three times previously; 24 percent were classed as occasional offenders; 12 percent were listed as first offenders, and 1 percent as accidental offenders. The crimes which this group had committed prior to their apprehension were: larceny, 30.7 percent; burglary, 21.7 percent; robbery, 9.8 percent; assault, 7.6 percent; homicide, 7.4 percent; rape, 5.4 percent; sodomy, 5.4 percent; other crimes, 13.1 percent.

The institution has had psychiatric and psychological service from the first. A rather unusual development is a group therapy program, managed with great interest by the inmates. While Napanoch is prepared to hold any inmate for life if necessary, the institution nevertheless gives every man his chance to prove that his return to community life on a parole status is warranted after a period of training.

Treatment is based on scientific classification, segregation in homogeneous groups, and an individualized plan of care best suited to the men's needs, aptitudes, and interests.

Industrial training is afforded in the various shops of the institution for the majority of the inmates. The industrial work includes the making or repairing of shoes, clothing, mattresses, brooms, sheet metal work, as well as cabinet making, blacksmithing, and printing. An aluminum shop turns out excellent utensils used in institutions under management of the state.

The visitor to these departments is impressed with the fact that this training is not on any amateur basis, but is for the most part, in respect to machinery and equipment, and quality and quantity of production, on a real industrial level. Many of the inmates find occupation on the institution farm, and for those who have advanced to the point where they are under consideration for parole, a farm colony is provided three miles from the institution, where their suitability for return to community life can be more fully tested.

The education program includes the usual school subjects and also health study, citizenship, and current events.

Every able-bodied inmate participates in military training in which a cadet may earn promotion and special privileges. Recreation is provided by such sports as baseball, basketball, volley ball and table tennis. The institution has a thirty-piece band, glee club and church choirs.

Great power of discretion is vested in the superintendent, subject to such regulations as the State Commissioner of Correction may establish, as to parole or discharge. The law permits parole and each year Napanoch has paroled a certain number of its inmates. Relatively few are discharged from parole, as it is the general policy of the institution to maintain the parole status indefinitely. Thus the paroled men are made to realize that they are at large on good behavior only, and that they are subject at any time to immediate return to the institution without formality.

VIRGINIA In 1926, in accordance with legislative enactment of that year, Virginia opened a state farm for defective misdemeanants. It provides for many types. The majority of the inmates are received by transfer from prisons and jails throughout the state. There is also provision, however, for the transfer of misdemeanants from the hospitals for the mentally ill, colonies for the mentally deficient, and industrial schools.

The farm receives both felons and delinquents, but the majority of defective misdemeanants are in buildings separated by the James River from the housing for more serious offenders.

A variety of activities, such as farming and mechanical trades, provide training. The manufacture of hand made brick and operation of the cannery are the primary industries. Surplus brick and canned produce are used wherever needed by other state agencies.

Some years after the farm was opened a service for women defective delinquents was established at the State Industrial Farm for Women. Academic training is offered from the first grade through high school. Vocational training includes many branches.

CONNECTICUT In Connecticut the 1939 Session of the General Assembly passed a law for segregation of defective delinquents. It was never made effective and was repealed when a new bill to plan an institution to accommodate them was passed in 1957.

Such special control of defective delinquents as has been described is in line with the newer approach to mental deficiency problems. It indicates the trend away from generalizations about mental defectives as a class, and recognizes that the retarded present many differences among themselves and cannot properly be spoken of or dealt with in general terms. Such a policy, instead of condemning all mental defectives and treating them uniformly as antisocial beings, demanding lifelong custodial

x. *Changing Concepts of Causation*

THE "Hill Folk" study of Davenport and Danielson, published in 1912, yielded data that did not bear out the "first law of heredity" enunciated previously by Dr. Davenport.[1] According to Dr. Davenport's original statement and the unit character theory, the proportion of defective offspring that could be expected from a number of matings of two persons regarded as definitely subnormal should be 100 percent, but the study showed that the proportion was only 77.3 percent.

The findings of Davenport and Danielson, and the hypothesis they advanced, foreshadowed the modern concept of heredity. This hypothesis is that mental deficiency, instead of being a definite entity which may be inherited as a unit Mendelian character (the absence of a single determiner for normality) is rather a composite term for varying complexes of traits exhibiting themselves in different kinds of deficiencies. Others supported these views and it became generally accepted that cases of inheritance due to one-factor differences (simple Mendelian cases) were limited chiefly to physical abnormalities or peculiarities, such as albinism, night-blindness, brachydactyly and other digital malformations, color-blindness, or hemophilia.

In the last fifty years, hundreds of studies have enlarged the understanding of genetics as applied to man. Further research will doubtless throw light on problems yet unsolved.

Dr. Curt Stern has given a clear presentation of current thought in his *Principles of Human Genetics*. The agents by which hereditary differences are transmitted are the nuclei of cells. Within the nuclei thread-like structures of various shapes are found. These are called chromosomes, because they take stains

[1] C. B. Davenport and F. H. Danielson, *The Hill Folk*.

intensively (Greek: *chromos*, color; *soma*, body). As the cell matures the chromosomes duplicate themselves and are found in identical pairs within each cell. In man each mature sperm and each egg has twenty-four pairs of chromosomes. The fertilized egg therefore has forty-eight pairs, one set derived from the mother, the other from the father. Different races such as white, negro, and Mongolian (and also the chimpanzee) have the same number of chromosomes.

Each chromosome is made up of a series of special materials arranged along its length. These materials are called genes, and these are the basis of hereditary traits. Each individual has a pair of each kind of chromosome, alike in arrangement of genes, so that each gene in an individual is represented twice. As Dr. Stern explains, the two pairs of any given gene in an individual may be compared to twins, and the total of all genes of an individual may be compared to a population made up of twins. Estimates indicate that there may be at least 1,000 genes per chromosome. This would mean that the cells of the body, having two assortments of genes, have 24,000 pairs.

The number of possible combinations of genes in the new individual is almost beyond calculation. The process which sorts and recombines the genetic contribution of the parents has been compared to the shuffling of cards. This explains why each child born to the same parents (identical twins excepted) is different from others in numerous genetic traits. The genes which the child does not inherit may be important too. Half of one person's genes are never transmitted, and this halving process goes on in each generation.

The tremendous range in the possible combinations of genes is not the end of nature's wizardry. It is believed that most traits or "characters" come about by the complex interaction of numerous genes. A "character" may be defined as any observable feature of the developing or fully developed individual, such as a biochemical property, anatomical structure, organ function, or mental characteristic. Dr. Stern points out that:

(1) no simple connection exists between most characters and a single gene; and (2) a single gene will often influence more than a single character.

On the other hand, sometimes several specific abnormal traits present in the same individual are transmitted as a unit. Such a group of characteristics is called a syndrome. How one gene may be responsible for such diverse characters is obscure, but it may be that some single primary genetic activity has manifold consequences. The existence of syndromes proves that a gene may produce effects in different parts of the body.

Differences in the action of genes during development are the basis of dominance and recessiveness. A single dominant gene may cause the appearance of an inherited trait and studies show that both dominant and recessive genetic contributions may result in mental deficiency.

Dr. Frank Lorimer summarizes the generally accepted view of the role of genes: "Many genes, perhaps hundreds, are involved in the genesis of the complex structure of cerebral tissues and the biochemical conditions involved in cerebral metabolism and in the volume and direction of chemico-electric currents, the organic basis of intelligence." He notes also that the whole structure may be made ineffective by any one of several adverse genetic or enviromental factors, and that many genetic and environmental factors must be positively coordinated in the making of intelligence.[2]

The complex interactions of the genes that finally produce the completed individual are not carried on in a sealed compartment unaffected by surrounding conditions. The environment plays an important part in the developmental process, and under differing conditions the same set of genes will produce different results. Experiment has shown, for example, that certain hereditary abnormalities in fruit flies are regularly passed on from generation to generation if moist air conditions prevail, but are not passed on when the air is kept comparatively dry.

[2] "Trends in Capacity for Intelligence," *Eugenical News* (June, 1952).

Earlier Views Reconsidered

Modern studies on heredity have naturally resulted in a re-examination of the data presented in the published histories of the "royal lines" of defective stock. The Kallikak family history, as the most famous of all, has come in for the most searching scrutiny. The findings and conclusions of this study have been sharply challenged. Many questions are raised by the almost too-perfect contrast between the two lines of descendants of Martin Kallikak Sr. How could the girl with whom Kallikak Sr. had had an illicit affair be reliably diagnosed as deficient after the lapse of more than a hundred years? How could a trustworthy diagnosis of her several hundred descendants be made? Most of them were dead by the time the study was made, and no case records of the modern type with their I.Q. ratings were available. Hearsay evidence had to be relied upon and one gains the impression that if this hearsay gave a picture of the individual as being shiftless, alcoholic, a "ne'er-do-well" or a criminal, the label of "feeblemindedness" was likely to be applied to him.

The Kallikak family history fitted well into the theories of inheritance of mental deficiency that were current at that time. In the light of the latest knowledge on this subject, however, it seems too tailor-made. In the realm of things human, judging from what is now known of hereditary mechanisms, family histories do not follow such invariably true courses, almost all bad on the one side, and almost all good on the other.

When Dr. Davenport's first law of inheritance was set forth in 1911 on the basis of Goddard's data, the inheritance of mental defect appeared quite general, definite and easily predictable. Therefore, programs of social control with the eugenic note uppermost were advocated with the greatest confidence as to the genetic results, even to the point of holding out the hope of substantially reducing the number of the subnormal in the next generation or two. To arrive at a solution of the problems of mental deficiency, it apparently remained only to apply measures such as sterilization, supplemented by complete segregation of those not sterilized, on a wide enough scale, to prevent procreation of this class. In contrast, the recent contributions to genetic science so emphasize the range of possibilities that may result from the combination of the genes of two parent individuals, and from the influence of varying environmental conditions, that the result cannot be accepted as a foregone conclusion.

The contrast between the older and newer views on the subject of heredity, marked as it is, should not be overdrawn. No exponent of the newer views would wish to obscure the fact that some forms of retardation do tend to run in certain families. That the basis of poor intelligence may be inherited in certain cases must be fully recognized.

Trends in Research

Dr. J. A. Fraser Roberts, speaking at the International Congress of Psychiatry in Paris in 1951, remarked that views of genetics have not changed substantially since 1944. There has been less writing on the subject since that time, perhaps because workers feel that it is more profitable to concentrate on nongenetic factors. He believes the greatest single advance in understanding causes of mental deficiency came with the recognition that there are two types. The first depends on a continuously graded character, general intelligence, and comprises the bulk of high grade defectives. The second, comprising the great bulk of the lower grade, depends on a highly diverse collection of entities, sometimes genetically determined, sometimes environmentally, sometimes by interaction of genetic and nongenetic factors.

Dr. Herman Yannet (Southbury Training School, Connecticut), reviewing progress of research since about 1940, also stresses the growing interest in the organic approach.[3] Some of the attempts to attack possible causes of mental deficiency have proved disappointing. It is now well established that treatment,

[3] See *American Journal of Mental Deficiency* (January, 1953).

for example, with glutamic acid, surgery to increase the blood supply to the brain, and compounds such as "nerve vitamins," are ineffective.

Dr. Yannet points out that the majority of children with mental deficiency owe the abnormality to influences operating at various times before birth. The prevention of such conditions would be more effective than any "magic bullet" applied after the condition is established. Among adverse prenatal conditions he mentions are prenatal infections, sensitizing blood factors, premature birth, and congenital malformations.

Letchworth Village has won an international reputation in the field of research through its Clinical Laboratories and the brilliant work of Dr. George A. Jervis, the Director. Although the research department was opened in 1921, it had to depend on private gifts for maintenance until the institution could include costs in current budgets.

In 1951 the New York state legislature made an initial appropriation of $25,000 for research at Letchworth Village. This official recognition of research was considered by the Senior Director, Dr. Harry C. Storrs, the most important event in the institution's history since its establishment. It was the first time that state funds had been specifically allocated for research in mental deficiency, and the appropriation was hailed by scientific workers everywhere as setting an example for similar action in other states.

Long before this grant Dr. Jervis, sometimes with collaborators, sometimes alone, had explored many obscurities in the intricate relationship of mind and body. Well over sixty reports have come from his laboratory on such subjects as phenylpyruvic idiocy, lipoidosis of the nervous system, diffuse sclerosis, pre-senile dementia, mongolism, allergic encephalitis, and brain damage.

Of chief interest to us are his extensive studies on inherited biochemical deficiencies. It appears, for example, that some types of mental deficiency are caused by inability of the body properly to metabolize proteins, vitamins, minerals, or other substances. In such cases faulty metabolism has caused mental deficiency in the parent and, if passed on, may give rise to mental retardation in the child. Thus what the child inherits is not mental deficiency, per se, but a faulty mechanism which does not provide for normal cerebral development. With expanded facilities, Dr. Jervis sees among fruitful fields for continued research such subjects as the pathological study of the brain, endocrine dysfunction, metabolic disturbances, and noxious agents affecting the mother during gestation. The New York State Research Institute for Mental Retardation, authorized in 1958, will be the first of its kind in the country. It will conduct "studies into the causes, nature and treatment of mental retardation—to discover and apply more efficient measures of prevention care and treatment."

The limited funds available for research have been everywhere a barrier to progress. Authorities believe that 10 percent of the operating cost of mental institutions should be assigned to research on causes, but as a rule, laboratories have to operate as best they can with no ticketed funds. When substantial support becomes available, faster progress can be expected. Another forward step will be better coordination of studies made in different parts of this and in other countries.

Research has revealed a much larger proportion of nonhereditary types of mental retardation originating from a variety of causes outside the germ-plasm than were formerly known to exist. Of the more recently known nonhereditary causes, three have come especially to notice. The most publicized is the "Rh factor," so called because it was first identified in the blood of a Rhesus monkey. If this factor is present in the blood of the unborn child but absent in the blood of the mother, a disturbance is set up which may result in damage to the nervous system of the unborn child. This war between blood that is Rh positive and blood that is Rh negative does not usually become destructive during gestation of the first child. The first born of parents whose blood is not alike in Rh factor is usually normal, while later children may show mental defect or other serious damage. Modern medical practice counters the danger to some extent by transfusing blood of the needed type.

Another discovery well covered by writers is that German measles and probably other disorders in the mother during pregnancy may cause mental deficiency in the child. Immunization of mothers susceptible to destructive infections may become an established precautionary measure.

Cerebral palsy is now known to be frequently accompanied by mental deficiency. A revealing article by Dr. Maurice Fouracre and Ellen A. Thiel [4] discusses the high incidence of retardation among sufferers from this condition. It cites a number of studies made in different parts of the country leading to estimates that of school age children with cerebral palsy, 25–30 percent are so handicapped mentally as not to be eligible for present school programs, and 40–50 percent, though educable, have intelligence below the average. In four studies mentioned, including 1,741 children, about 70 percent were found to have I.Q.s below 90.

The painstaking research in hundreds of laboratories is expected to disclose other causes of mental deficiency. A study of the possible origin of retardation in "molecular diseases" is being made at the California Institute of Technology under Dr. Linus Pauling with a grant from the Ford Foundation. Another authority states that causes are so numerous that they "cover almost the whole field of injurious agents and processes to which human beings are exposed." The relation of sociocultural factors, poor environment, and severe deprivation to retardation has been explored by Dr. S. B. Sarason and Dr. Thomas Gladwin. Dr. Richard L. Masland has made an extensive survey of research for the National Association for Retarded Children.[5] His summaries show promising progress toward understanding many factors that may cause mental retardation.

This discussion of heredity may be briefly summarized. It is believed that in less than half of the cases, inheritance of faulty genes plays a role in the causation of mental deficiency. The

[4] "Education of Children with Mental Retardation Accompanying Cerebral Palsy," *American Journal of Mental Deficiency*, January, 1953.

[5] Seymour B. Sarason, and Thomas Gladwin, "Psychological and Cultural Problems in Mental Subnormality: A Review of Research," and R. L. Masland, "The Prevention of Retardation: A Survey of Research," in *American Journal of Mental Deficiency* (May, 1958).

expanding field of research on nonhereditary causes promises to reduce the incidence of mental deficiency not hereditary in origin. Some of these causes are now amenable to treatment, and means of conquering others will doubtless be found. At present science is nearer to prevention than it is to cure.

Substantial sums have now been appropriated, notably by the National Institute of Mental Health, for long-term research on the causes of mental retardation and cerebral palsy. Extensive study of causes will undoubtedly eventually lead to reducing the incidence of retardation and will perhaps open the way to successful treatment.

New Data on Fecundity

As we saw earlier a persistent bugaboo which has been the motif of more than one alarmist book and numerous articles has been based on the popular belief that the retarded are extremely prolific and are outrunning normal stocks in rate of reproduction so rapidly as to threaten to inherit the earth. Critical examination of this formerly widely held view indicates that it is not well founded.

Dr. A. Myerson's studies showed that many individuals whose retardation was apparently of genetic origin were of such low grade, mentally and physically, that the males were not capable of sexual intercourse, and the fertility of the females was doubtful. Myerson concluded that among this group, "there is a strong tendency to race extinction due to the very low physical and mental level." [6]

In some of the earlier studies, Dr. Goddard showed that in the families of the hereditary group at Vineland, including earlier generations as well as the present, the number of children per mating, who survived infancy, was 3.8. In the Nam family the average number of children of the reproducing married women was shown to be 4.025; in the Juke family, 4.306. If the Juke figure is revised to include married women who were barren, the

[6] *Inheritance of Mental Diseases* (Baltimore, Williams & Wilkins, 1925).

average number of children per female was 3.526. The Nam figure would need to be similarly reduced to allow for sterile marriages.

Data on the size of families represented by institutional cases were supplied by the Myerson study of a large series of cases at Waverley and Wrentham. The figures given are exclusive of still-births, and are based both on complete and incomplete families. At Waverley the average number of children in families from which the patients came was 3.8; the average Wrentham family was 4.5. It was shown by Dr. Myerson that the Wrentham family was slightly larger than that in the general population of Massachusetts, but no larger than that of families on the cultural level from which the patients came. Dr. Myerson believed that the slightly higher birth rate of the Wrentham families was explained therefore not by their deficiency but by the cultural level from which they came, as birth rate varies inversely with the cultural level. In two-thirds of the Wrentham cases, the patient was the only member of the family who was subnormal. The size of families in these studies is not alarmingly large.

Dr. J. E. W. Wallin traced the siblings of public school children of all ranges of intelligence coming to the St. Louis Psycho-Educational Clinic, and ascertained the average number of children in the families represented by these 4,324 siblings. He found that the families in which there were retarded children had an average excess of .063 child per mating, as compared with the general average of the entire group. The families with only normal or slightly retarded children had an average of 1.2 children less than the families in which there were mental defectives.

These St. Louis figures indicate a somewhat higher birth rate among families in which there is at least one retarded child. Wallin cites a great deal of evidence, however, to show that the survival rate among subnormals is appreciably less than among normals, both with respect to infant mortality and the mortality in childhood and later years, indicating that the lower rate of survival of the mentally defective may balance the differential in birth rate.

In connection with the survey of 10,455 retarded children in the public schools of Massachusetts, Dr. Neil A. Dayton [7] found that the number of children born to native white mothers of all ages in families having a mentally defective child was 3.3, in families having a mildly retarded child 3.2, and in families representing the general native white population, 2.8.

Modern research confirms such findings. Studies in England [8] indicate that among the moderately retarded fecundity is rare, and among the severely retarded almost completely absent. Among the high grade the question is still unsettled. It was noted that greatest fertility occurred when parents had a mean I.Q. of about 80 or 90. Below this families were smaller. The English writers call attention to the fact that measurement of effective fertility associated with any given intelligence level depends on ascertaining the number of people who have no children at all, as well as the viability of offspring. In one survey of offspring of certified mental defectives, the proportion of children who died under one year was about double that of the general population.

The Rhode Island Mental Deficiency Register for 1950 gives interesting figures, though it is pointed out that limitations of the data must be considered in drawing conclusions. Of 6,676 names listed, a total of 886 individuals had one or more children at that time. The number of offspring was 2,151, an average of between 2 and 3 per parent. The entries under "married" showed the number of children to be very similar to that in the general population.

In the light of such data as are available, the assertion that mentally defective stocks are propagating at such a rapid rate that they threaten to swamp civilization appears to belong to the legends of the past.

When allowances are made for the large number of retarded persons who will never reproduce because of sexual sterility or unattractiveness, and for the others who are prevented from reproducing because of being segregated in institutions, it would

[7] Neil A. Dayton, "Order of Birth and Size of Family," *American Journal of Psychiatry*, 8:979–1005.
[7] L. S. Penrose, *The Biology of Mental Defect*.

appear that the mentally deficient are scarcely holding their own in the general population.

Regarding the whole question of the inheritance of mental deficiency there is only one thing of which we can be certain at present, and that is of our uncertainty. The existing knowledge on the subject merely indicates the importance of further research. The one observation that can be safely made is that the hereditary transmission of retardation is neither so simple, nor so predictable, nor so alarming numerically, as was formerly believed.

XI. New Light on Behavior

THE old portrayal of the social sins of the mentally handicapped, discussed in Chapter VI, shows but one side of mental deficiency—the worst shortcomings of the most seriously delinquent and incompetent. It is far from being the whole picture. And yet, until recently, hasty and unfounded generalizations concerning the propensities of the retarded as a whole have been drawn from such cases whose very failure brought them to public notice, while other peaceful thousands who never got into trouble were entirely overlooked. These old ideas still color the thinking of many people.

A study of case histories reveals that many of the retarded in institutions, from whose numbers most statistics as to the relation of mental deficiency to delinquency have been drawn, come from wretched environments. Because this type often falls into social misconduct, it has not been uncommon to think of mental defectives in general as predestined to lives of crime and delinquency, instead of considering their behavior, when faulty, as for the most part the product of a bad environment.

In his article on "Backward and Defective Children," Dr. Pearce Bailey said:

Half the cases which appear before the New York City Children's Court are brought there on account of improper guardianship, which means that they have no home life at all, or that their home surroundings are such as to turn into criminals any but the strongest characters. In such surroundings, being credulous and imitative, they take on the ways of the adults with whom they are thrown.[1]

In a statistical analysis of 4,000 young repeated offenders, consisting of 2,000 offenders studied in Chicago between 1909 and

[1] Bailey, Backward and Defective Children, pp. 1–2.

1915, and 2,000 offenders studied in Boston from 1917 to 1923, Dr. William Healy and Dr. Augusta Bronner [2] found that 13.5 percent of the group were clearly subnormal. But Drs. Healy and Bronner further found through their follow-up work with mentally handicapped delinquents that environment had largely determined the outcome, and they asserted that when the mentally subnormal are properly cared for, they do not develop criminal tendencies.

Dr. Healy stated that "it is impossible to explain delinquency in terms of a numerical intelligence quotient." In other words, although a somewhat larger percentage of the mentally deficient may drift into delinquency, this does not mean that there is any causal connection between deficiency per se and delinquency per se, but rather that mental defectives, frequently coming from poor environments and being deprived of opportunities for wholesome contacts, are more likely to come under influences that will lead them into delinquent ways.

A former director of the Institute for Child Guidance in New York City, Dr. Lawson G. Lowrey,[3] stated that, in child guidance clinics operating over a period of five or more years in certain cities, mental deficiency has been found to be a lesser factor in difficult behavior than was anticipated. In surveying pupils of typical schools in Minneapolis and Cleveland, some correlation was found between behavior difficulties and intelligence "in the sense that those children who on intelligence depart in either direction from the average, present a larger number of behavior problems than does the group with the average intelligence. . . . Furthermore, in individual cases behavior problems of the feeble-minded child may differ neither in kind nor degree from those of a highly superior child."

---

[2] Healy and Bronner, *Delinquents and Criminals: Their Making and Unmaking* (New York, Macmillan, 1926), p. 149, ff.

[3] Lowrey, "The Relationship of Feeblemindedness to Behavior Disorders," *Journal of Psycho-Asthenics*, 33:96-100.

Multiple Factors in Delinquency

Dr. Lowrey explained the behavior tendencies of certain of the mentally deficient in terms of a "conflict over difference, or if one prefers the term, inferiority complex." The deficient child's attempt to compensate for his intellectual limitations, which cause him to fail in competition, may manifest itself in difficult behavior. Such mechanisms, however, Dr. Lowrey said, are not confined to the mentally deficient, but occur in children of average or superior intelligence, resulting from difficulties of any other kind, such as physical handicaps, home difficulties, or sense of social inferiority. He concluded "that intelligence is only one of many factors which may produce objectionable reactions, and that factors of personality, the integration of the emotional and instinctive life, and in the social situation, are far more important than the mere question of intelligence."

Studies of the relation of retardation to crime and delinquency have very generally been made of selected groups, those in custodial institutions, in prisons and reformatories, or in houses of prostitution. Naturally, in such groups there is found to be a large proportion of deficiency, as the offenders who are detained are the "caught" ones and the most stupid. Their cleverer comrades are quick enough to slip through the fingers of the law. It is usually the criminal of normal or superior intelligence who is the instigator and who uses the subnormal as his dupes.

Studies of the mental status of 3,206 inmates of county jails and penitentiaries made in connection with surveys conducted by the former National Committee for Mental Hygiene in various parts of the country showed nearly 14 percent of the entire group to be afflicted with mental defect, while an additional 6.6 percent were noted as having borderline intelligence. In a study made under the same auspices, of 1,216 male and female offenders in thirty-four county jails and penitentiaries in New York, 7.6 percent were found to be deficient and an additional 5.4 percent were found to have borderline intelligence. These figures show that while the retarded, as would naturally be expected, constitute a substantial percentage of all delinquent groups, they are by no means responsible for the bulk of crime and delinquency, but a rather small proportion of it. In interpreting such figures, again allowance must always be made for the fact that the subnormal delinquents are the ones most likely to be apprehended and convicted, and thus any such group under observation is more or less selected. Dr. Bronner was convinced that the rate of delinquency among the retarded was low, even in 1914, the very time when all the sweeping assertions were being made about the high percentage of retardation among delinquents, after she found upon studying more than 500 cases of delinquency, that the retarded represented only 10 percent.

Dr. Fernald, on analyzing the results of a study of 5,000 mentally defective school children in Massachusetts from nine to sixteen years of age, found that less than 8 percent of the entire group gave any indication of antisocial or troublesome behavior.[4]

Later studies reflect the modern concept of delinquency which rejects the idea of unitary causes and focuses on personality frustration and multiple factors. For example, a study of 1,610 prisoners at the Washington State Penitentiary, showed only about 1 percent definitely subnormal. The data appeared to confirm the fact that many factors are at work in causing delinquent behavior of which mental deficiency is only one.

Bovet has summarized findings of many authorities on the relation of intelligence to delinquency.[5] He points out that in different parts of the world there are varying views on classification, such as to age and degree. What is considered delinquency in one country may not be so classified in another. He calls attention also to the fact that the distinction between delinquent and nondelinquent is not only arbitrary but is based on quantitative rather than qualitative factors. Personality and social factors may, by their intensity of degree, cause an individual to be classed as a delinquent while the usual psychological examination would show little or nothing to distinguish him from a nondelinquent.

---

[4] Fernald, *Journal of Psycho-Asthenics*, 29:213.
[5] L. Bovet, "Psychiatric Aspects of Juvenile Delinquency," World Health Organization Monograph, Series No. 1 (Geneva, 1951).

Among writers cited by Bovet are those below:

Chassel, after a survey of literature in 1935
The relation is positive but low.

Healy and Bronner in New Light on Delinquency and Its Treatment, *New Haven, 1936*
The intelligence level does not in general distinguish the delinquent from his nondelinquent sibling, though it may have importance . . . in individual cases.

Exner, German authority writing in 1939
The correlation is barely significant and by no means implies a relation of cause and effect.

Stein, psychiatrist to Chicago Juvenile Court, reporting on 705 juvenile delinquents seen in 1947
The probable distribution of intelligence among juveniles labeled delinquent is the same as, if not higher than for nondelinquents.

Cyril Burt in The Young Delinquent, *London, 1948*
My own percentages reveal among delinquents a proportion of mental defectives five times as great as among the school population at large.

Pearce, in a report at the Scientific Conference, London, 1949
It seems definite that the intelligence of the average delinquent is considerably less than that of the nondelinquent.

In quoting the experts against each other, it is not intended to underrate any of them. It is rather to show what should by now be obvious—that opinions differ, that much further research is needed, that the results of studies now in the files should be somewhat discounted because of their selective nature.

The Glueck Studies

Some of the most illuminating work in the understanding of delinquency has been contributed by Dr. and Mrs. Sheldon Glueck. In one of their earlier studies they compared the intelligence of 1,000 juvenile delinquents who had passed through the Boston Juvenile Court and who had been studied at the Judge Baker Foundation Clinic, with that of 2,800 Boston school children studied by the Psycho-Educational Clinic of Harvard University.[6] At the top of the scale 41.6 percent of the delinquents had I.Q.s of 91 and over, while 79 percent of school children were in this range. At the lower end of the scale, 13.1 percent of delinquents were classed as defective (I.Q. 70 and below) while only 1.5 percent of the school children fell in this category.

Their later books, *Unraveling Juvenile Delinquency* and *Delinquents in the Making,* describe fascinating research. A study was made of 500 persistently misbehaving boys closely matched as to general intelligence, age, and ethnic origin, with 500 law-abiding boys. All came from underprivileged areas. On the Wechsler-Bellevue Full Scale Intelligence Test the average intelligence of the delinquents was found to rate 92. In the control group the average I.Q. was 94.

The components that make up general intelligence were analyzed, as largely determined by the Wechsler-Bellevue and partly by the Rorschach tests. On verbal aspects (those dealing with the use of abstract symbols, such as vocabulary, information, logical reasoning, and comprehension of problems) the delinquents made a slightly poorer showing than the nondelinquents. It is noted, however, that the difference may not have been a real one, since environment may influence such tests. Thus the vocabulary test, though a good index of general intelligence, is somewhat affected by the amount of schooling, and delinquents are often truants and retarded in school. The information test also is affected by educational opportunity and the delinquents on the whole had had fewer advantages than the nondelinquents.

On performance aspects of the scale, designed to test intellectual function involved in handling concrete material rather than abstract ideas, the delinquent group rated lower on some, higher on others, but on the whole were found somewhat superior. The nondelinquents were stronger in abstract thinking and generalizations.

On the quantitative-dynamic aspects of intellectual function, as shown by Rorschach tests, there was little difference between

[6] *One Thousand Juvenile Delinquents* (Harvard University Press, 1934).

the groups in originality, creativity, intuition, and some other fields. There was, however, a significantly greater proportion of delinquents than of controls who were unrealistic thinkers, lacking in common sense, and unmethodical in approaching mental problems. They were found less able to adjust to the realistic demands of life.

In emotional adequacy only half as many delinquents as others (15 percent compared to 31 percent) were found able to conduct or express themselves with fair efficiency. On the other hand, the delinquent group contained twice as many boys (28 percent compared to 14 percent) found dynamic, forceful, and energetic. There were three times as many delinquents as controls who were markedly aggressive, a trait which, if undirected, may lead to trouble. There were also more extroverts among the delinquents, of the type who leap before they look. On suggestibility, delinquents showed a frequency of 60 percent as compared to 26 percent, and on stubbornness 41 percent compared to 8 percent of the controls.

The Gluecks concluded that the emotional handicaps of the delinquent are serious. They found, however, that low intelligence is not among the more significant factors that produce delinquency.

In making a fair estimate of the percentage of mental defect among delinquents, an important factor to be considered is that not infrequently the low score of an individual in the tests may be due not to mental deficiency, but to emotional factors resulting from the attitude of the offender toward his apprehension or imprisonment. There may be lack of cooperation, language difficulty, fear that the tests are of an inquisitional character, or the feeling that they are not to be taken seriously. In other words, when the mental age is found to be below normal, that fact in itself cannot always be taken as evidence of mental deficiency because of these other factors which may affect the result of the tests.

It is not intended here to obscure or deny the tendency of a proportion of the retarded to fall into social difficulties. That would be contrary to common observation and the findings of scientific studies. What it is desired to bring out is, first, that the social indictment of this group as set forth in Chapter VI was grossly overdrawn; second, that there is apparently no inborn or universal or necessary connection between inferior intelligence and social offenses, such as early hasty generalizations made out. The mentally deficient probably contribute more than their due proportion to social offenders, not because of any direct relationship between limited intelligence and social misbehavior, but because they are more likely to be underprivileged, coming as they often do, from homes lacking good parental guidance, decent housing, adequate economic resources, and a wholesome neighborhood environment. They are thus naturally put in the way of unfavorable influences to which, as suggestible persons with limited powers of independent thought, they are more likely than others to succumb. That most of the mentally deficient have no innate propensities toward evil-doing is shown by the results obtained when society puts good, rather than bad influences in their way.

Part Two: Modern Programs
Rehabilitation

XII. *The Modern Institution*

THE custodial type of institutional care urged by the advocates of complete segregation has been likened to a still lake which receives a slow influx of new waters and loses its contents only by gradual evaporation. Such an institution slowly receives patients as its capacity permits, and keeps them until death takes them away. Even if custodial care for all were desirable, it would entail enormous expenditures. No state has provided institutional facilities for more than a fraction of its retarded. To the rest, the institution has had to shut its eyes. It has been a case of giving costly care to one and letting some nine others drift.

Homer Folks, then Secretary of the State Charities Aid Association, writing of the institutional program in New York in 1914, showed how such a situation had developed:

The institution at ———, for instance, has regarded itself as charged with the duty of receiving a small number of feebleminded women, free from disease . . . and of maintaining a quiet, orderly, spacious, presentable resort. . . . It apparently has never lifted up its eyes to look over the State and behold all those other feeblminded young women who are in imminent danger in almshouses. . . . In other words, ——— has been thinking of itself as an institution, of its laundry, its routine, its external appearance—not of the real, substantial, underlying needs of the State which it was established to serve.

The truth which faced those broad-visioned workers who insisted upon seeing the problem as a whole was not a dream of how well the situation might be controlled if there were permanent institutional care for all; it was rather a case of facing the plain fact that, despite valiant effort the segregation program had not and probably never would be realized. It was a question therefore of making the existing institutions of the greatest possible service within the limits of their capacity. To go back to the simile, the newer conception of the institution is that of a lake fed and drained by a running stream, with ample inflow and outflow. Such an institution is not for custodial care primarily (although certain cases will of course need such care), but rather for training and finally restoring to society all those capable of social adjustment.

The followers of Seguin had opened the first schools for the retarded in this country with sanguine hopes of curing or so greatly improving their charges that they could take their places in society after their "education" had been completed. We have seen how this hope was blasted and how these institutions subsequently became largely custodial in character. With the discovery of the "moron," however, the institutions, which had formerly existed for the care of the lower grade, began to receive an increasing proportion of these higher grade cases.

Here was a different proposition from that which confronted the early institutions. They were now given material to work with that was at the same time more troublesome and more hopeful. And the approach to the care of this material was not primarily by the method of physiological education with the hope of curing mental defect, as in the old days, but rather by the method of social education. Recognizing the futility of attempting to increase the intelligence, the more progressive institutions sought to develop those personal traits and social capacities, which even in the retarded were found to be capable of growth through training. Where sad experience had said to Howe and Wilbur, "You cannot intellectualize," the leaders of the modern school have replied, "Very well, then, we will socialize."

The Training Program

It is customary, when patients first arrive, to place them in the hospital or reception building for several weeks. This is a precaution against the possible spread of contagious diseases, such as measles. During this period a thorough physical and mental check-up is made. An effort is made to put every patient into good physical condition and remedial work is begun on defects that yield to treatment.

The next step is a careful study of abilities and disabilities, such as speech defects. The psychological laboratory offers a wide variety of tests, and results guide the placement of the patient in ward, school, and occupation. Re-testing at intervals is the general rule and serves to gauge progress or to channel training in a new direction. For older patients the Vocational Department will direct appropriate work.

The Social Service interviews relatives as soon as possible, and begins a friendly contact that may last for years. Personal and family history are used by the admissions staff, as at a clinic. Information on family background and personalities of people near the patient not only throws light on his present condition, but may also be a determining factor later, when release under supervision is considered. The importance of preserving the family unit is recognized. Relatives, if the patient has any, are encouraged to visit him on the regular visiting days, or may come at other times by arrangement.

The progressive institution carries on an active educational program even for severely retarded cases. The children receive constant and painstaking training in basic personal habits, such as care of the body, dressing and undressing, orderliness, table manners—in fact, everything that normal children of pre-school age are taught in their own homes. Sensory and motor development, hand training, and even walking are stimulated, with gymnastics, occupations, and play as far as possible in the open air. Speech training is also emphasized. No means is overlooked of developing in these lower grade children whatever capacity they possess for self-care, for personal comfort, and for activity and happiness.

As to the higher grade cases, the institution proceeds on the assumption that they are, if possible, to be made ready sooner or later for community life. Having these children and young people under its supervision twenty-four hours of the day, the institution makes everything in the daily program contribute toward the building of desirable social behavior, starting with such fundamentals as cleanliness and personal hygiene and leading on to the development of self-reliance, self-control, obedience, industry, thrift, and capacity for social intercourse. The steady routine, constant repetition, kindly discipline, and ordered group life which the institution provides are powerful forces in developing regular habits of the right kind. The typical mental defective, doing less thinking for himself than the normal person, largely relies upon habit for the determination of his activities from day to day, and if good habits are well enough established, he is not apt later to deviate from them.

School classes give such academic instruction as each child is capable of receiving. For the occupational training of the younger girls there are classes in domestic science, sewing, cooking, and household management, and also in the industrial pursuits of rug- and basket-making, and the operation of machines of the factory type, such as knitting machines for making stockings and sweaters. The older girls can pass on to training in practical nursing and to further training in cooking and laundry work as provided in the kitchens and laundry of the institution. For the occupational training of boys, there are painting, carpentry, die-making, broom- and brush-making, and the like. Following such preliminary training, the older and more capable boys assist the employed staff of the institution in the carpentry shop, bakery, storerooms, electric department, power-house, plumbing, and painting divisions. Farm and dairy work also provide practical vocational training for many boys who have an inclination in this direction. The wide variety of training experiences offered in a large state institution is one of its advantages over the smaller private institution.

Opportunities for recreation and amusement are furnished by story telling, supervised play, dances, motion pictures, dramatics, and entertainments given inside the institution, and for religious expression through the Sunday services conducted by the various faiths.

One of the best known institutions for mental defectives in this country is the Training School at Vineland, New Jersey, a privately supported, not a state, institution. Vineland, through the high standards of care and training which it has maintained, and through its extensive experimental and research work, has been a great teaching center and laboratory for the whole mental deficiency field. Under the leadership, for many years, of the beloved Edward R. Johnstone, the Training School has been permeated with the atmosphere of its motto, "Happiness first; all else follows."

The State School at Waverley, Massachusetts, the oldest state institution for mental defectives in the country, has been notable for its leadership throughout the hundred years of its existence. The principal reason for this leadership is revealed in the present official name of that institution: The Walter E. Fernald State School.

For thirty-seven years, from 1887 until his death in 1924, Dr. Walter Elmore Fernald gave to the State School and to its children—*his* children—an unstinted measure of personal as well as professional devotion. He combined in a rare way the human and the scientific. Coming into the work as a young physician within a decade of the passing of those three great pioneers, Seguin, Howe, and Wilbur, Dr. Fernald felt the quickening of the scientific interest and high-minded purpose which had animated these men, and carried on where they left off. Speaking always with the authority which comes from keen observation and sound judgment, and with the vision that marks the leader, Dr. Fernald's voice was heard throughout the nation and much of the world.

In Dr. Fernald's own writings and practice may be traced step by step the development of the changing attitudes and programs through which the mental deficiency movement has passed; naturally so, because he himself played so prominent a part in shaping the movement. He made himself heard as strongly as any other in warning as to the menace of the retarded, and the need for their complete segregation during the period of eugenic alarm. And his, again, was the first voice to be raised, with authority which carried conviction, in tempering these views, and showing the whole picture of mental deficiency as it is seen today.

After-Care Studies

One of the first published studies to attract general notice to the constructive possibilities of the institution was Dr. Fernald's "After-Care Study of the Patients Discharged from Waverley for a Period of Twenty-five Years," published in 1919. The great significance of this study lies in the fact that it includes cases which were discharged from the institution during the time when life-long segregation was believed to be the best policy. The majority of the cases were discharged under protest, against the advice of the institutional authorities. Quite a few were "runaways." A small number, however, were permitted to go because they had no antisocial tendencies. The total number of discharges for the twenty-five years was 1,537. The small number of discharges, with a census ranging from 640 in 1890 to 1,660 in 1914, shows that the policy of long continued segregation was consistently followed during the entire period. It was honestly believed that nearly all patients should remain in the institution indefinitely.

Of the 1,537 discharges, 891 were not included in the study, for the following reasons: 437 were transferred to other institutions, 175 were returned to other states, and 279 could not be located. The method of investigation consisted first in sending a circular letter to relatives or friends of the discharged patients asking for information. The social worker of the institution followed up these letters with personal visits to the family; she also talked with persons in the community such as ministers, social workers, and police authorities.

According to the concepts of mental deficiency that were prevalent at this time, disastrous social consequences were expected from sending these defective persons, especially the women, out into the world. Histories were obtainable on 176 discharged females. Of these, 27 had married, nearly all above the social level of their own parents. Eleven of these married women "were living useful and blameless lives and apparently were making good in every way." To these 11 women, 34 children were born. All of the children appeared normal. Three of the 11 women had been discharged from the institution without protest. The other eight had been discharged very much against the advice of the institution and only upon a writ of habeas corpus, yet they turned out unexpectedly well.

There was, of course, a debit side to the careers of the women. The other 16 married women had records of antisocial behavior and their marriages turned out poorly. All had been discharged under protest.

Of the total of 176 discharged women, 48 were found to have been sexually irregular after discharge. These 48 included the 16 married women mentioned above, 11 unmarried mothers who had borne in all 13 illegitimate children, and 21 others subsequently re-committed. In practically none of these cases were there responsible relatives or friends to give supervision. No record of venereal diseases was found except for four cases of syphilis. This is a surprisingly small percentage of 176, and indicates that these women were not great factors in the spread of social diseases.

Although 29 women of the 176 had been admitted to other institutions, only 4 of the entire group in the period of twenty-five years had been committed to correctional institutions.

On the economic side there could be counted as assets the 11 women who were making good as wives and home makers; 8 others who were supporting themselves, getting their own jobs and paying their own bills; and 32 who were capable workers at home to the extent of "earning their salt." Thus nearly 30 percent of the group were economic assets to the extent of at least earning their own way in the world.

This analysis of the records must be interpreted remembering that it was on the whole an unfavorable group to begin with. The results obtained under these inauspicious circumstances were little short of a revelation. That there was found among the women no preponderant amount of delinquency, so few illegitimate children, and so few children in general, that many were good wives, and that many more were materially contributing to their maintenance, was a result not altogether anticipated even by Dr. Fernald. In short, the findings lent little support to former sweeping statements about the general antisocial proclivities of the mentally deficient. Dr. Fernald hesitated for two years to publish the results of this study because they had seemed so much at variance with accepted theories.

In publishing the study, Dr. Fernald led the way to a fuller understanding of the social possibilities of the mentally deficient. With such results from an unselected and largely unfavorable group who had simply been "let go" without further supervision on the part of the institution, it at once became clear that there were hopeful possibilities for successfully restoring to the community cases carefully trained and carefully selected as having developed the qualities necessary for extra-institutional life. If, to training and selection, there were added a trial period on parole during which the former patient would have the close guidance and supervision of the institutional social worker, the program would be a promising one.

The findings of the same survey regarding discharged males were even more encouraging. The histories of 470 discharged males were obtained. Only 13 of the entire group had married. There were only 12 children to these marriages and all appeared to be normal. The homes of the married men were neat and clean and the children well behaved. Two of the married men who had been supporting their homes had been sent to the reformatory for larceny. The other 11 were included in a group of 28 high grade cases who were earning a good living without supervision. By occupation these 28 included teamsters, elevator men, laborers, factory hands, farm hands, soda clerks, tinsmiths. One of the men had saved $2,000, and another owned his own home.

One group, of 86 higher grade cases, had regular employment and lived at home under the close supervision of their families. The types of employment covered 39 occupations, as factory hand, painter, baker, laborer, printing pressman, freight handler, railroad brakeman, machinist, barber, etc. Only a few were common laborers. The behavior of these 86 was very satisfactory. They had been away from the school for an average of nine years, yet none had been sexually troublesome or evinced any delinquent tendencies. Steady work, good homes, and the careful supervision of relatives had enabled these former institutional patients to become useful and desirable members of society.

Another group, of 77 lower grade cases of various ages, were not working for wages, but were able to do some work at home. Eight were attending public school. "These persons all seemed to be harmless and inoffensive. . . . In this group also the lack of serious character defect and the fact that they were closely supervised were important factors in their good behavior."

A group of 59 cases, made up of a still lower grade type, consisted entirely of dependents. The report was quite favorable because the homes were good and the families were able to assume the burden of support and protection. In the last two groups mentioned, the cases which had proved troublesome had already been returned to the institution.

Only 24 of the men had been committed to penal institutions following their discharge. They were the defective delinquent type for whom, in those days, no special provision had been made. They had been at Waverley on an average of less than one year. Eleven had run away from the institution, 9 had been taken away by parents, and 4 had been discharged as unsuitable for the institution. In addition to these 24, 8 discharged boys had been sentenced to juvenile reformatories. Besides this total of 32 who had "served time," 23 others had been arrested for crimes or misdemeanors, but had not been committed to penal institutions.

Another group of 43 of the discharged males were committed to other institutions, such as hospitals for the mentally ill or epileptic. Sixty-eight others were readmitted to Waverley because they did not get on well or were a burden at home, or were not easily controlled.

To quote Dr. Fernald:

The results of this survey should be interpreted with great caution. . . . Still many unpromising cases did well. There was a surprisingly small amount of criminality and sex offense, and especially of illegitimacy. We may hope for a much better record when we have extra-institutional visitation and supervision of all discharged cases. . . . The survey shows that there are bad defectives and good defectives. It also shows that even some apparently bad do "settle down." . . . It is most important that the limited facilities for segregation should be used for the many who can be protected in no other way.

Consider one sentence of the above paragraph: "The survey shows that there are bad defectives and good defectives." That simple statement seems to be the key to the whole problem. Some of the retarded are apparently defective in social feeling and are unteachable in that regard; others have already become so well established in delinquency that to teach them differently requires long and painstaking effort. These are the type that should be selected for segregation and institutional care for an indefinite period, some of them in a special institution of the Bridgewater or Napanoch type.

But there is now recognized a much larger number of inherently "good" mental defectives, by nature affectionate, confiding, loyal, industrious, who crave respectability, who are anxious to be like other people, ready to seize the opportunity under guidance to make the most of themselves. They are in a sense always children, suggestible and easily led. Thus, the influences of a bad home and a bad neighborhood, the ridicule of society, the sense of being a social outcast, sometimes make of these people the subnormal social offender.

A study of the careers of those discharged from Letchworth Village confirmed the Waverley experience. Dr. H. C. Storrs, who reported this study, noted the same evolution as occurred at Waverley:

At the time of the opening of Letchworth Village in 1911, it was believed that all feebleminded were potential criminals, and that to protect the public against their acts, lifelong custodial care should be
provided for them. At that time also the belief in the hereditary etiol-
ogy of mental defect was strong and it was felt that society . . .
should be protected by holding the feebleminded in institutions to
prevent them from reproducing their own type.

As the population at Letchworth Village grew, conditions of overcrowding often developed and a more lenient attitude toward discharge was forced upon us, the justification of which was at times
questioned. We all agree that our ideas have changed . . . and we
now know that we cannot keep children of the higher mental grades
in an institution indefinitely.[1]

This study included males and females discharged from Letchworth Village prior to January 1, 1927. The total number discharged was 1,164 (males 766, females 398). Of these 1,164, there
were 548 not included: some had been transferred, while patients,
directly to other institutions; others died subsequent to discharge,
and the remainder could not be located or insufficient information concerning them was obtained. But the investigators were
able to locate and classify 616 (433 males and 183 females).
Of the males, some 73 percent were listed as successful and 27
percent as failures. Of the girls, nearly 75 percent were listed as
successful and 25 percent as failures.

In summing up the findings Dr. Storrs said: "It appears reasonably probable that the majority who are now successful will continue to be so and that the interests of society are practically as
well protected as if they had remained in the institution."

A thoughtful study of patients discharged from the St. Louis
State Training School was completed in 1953.[2] Its purpose was
to analyze the training program of the School as a preparation
for community living as well as of the after-care program. The
74 patients in the study (50 males and 24 females), employed

[1] Storrs, "A report on an Investigation Made of Cases Discharged from
Letchworth Village," *Journal of Psycho-Asthenics* 34:220-232.
[2] Edward C. Harold, "Employment of Patients Discharged from The St.
Louis State Training School," *American Journal of Mental Deficiency*
(January, 1955).

during 1953, had been discharged from the institution eight months to fourteen years. In I.Q. they ranged from 33 to 81; in age from fifteen to thirty-nine.

Of 29 employed in business and industry, only 12 had had assistance in obtaining their positions. Most of the jobs were of unskilled, semiskilled, clerical, or personal service nature. No correlation was found between either wages or type of work and the I.Q. Two-thirds of the group had held their positions for more than one year. Wages were somewhat below the national average for comparable work. Half the group carried life insurance and had saved money. A few were buying homes.

Of 45 patients employed in institutional or domestic work, nearly half had been referred to positions by the Training School. Nearly half were placed at work in religious institutions, where the setting offered some protection. Most of the jobs were of the personal service type. A high correlation was found between intelligence and the complexity of work performed. Four-fifths had remained in their jobs over one year; more than half from five to thirteen years. Two-thirds of the group had savings, the median being $625.

Among conclusions it was noted that (1) factors in success were good personality adjustment, the degree of guidance given, work assignments within adaptive capacity; (2) patients were better prepared for institution and domestic work than for industrial jobs, and more in-service training was given in the former; (3) earnings in business and industry were higher, but institutions and domestic jobs offered more protection and personal guidance; (4) the higher earning potential in industry suggested placing patients in such jobs when adequate vocational guidance and other services are available.

These studies have been described to show that even when institutions could offer little or no supervision, the paroled and discharged patients made records far exceeding expectations. The degree of success of even unpromising cases reflected the excellent training the patients had been given. The favorable findings gave rise to a new faith in the mentally deficient and paved the way for the extensive community services we know today.

Many other studies, such as that described in Chapter XV, have amply demonstrated that the trained mental defective can hold a creditable place outside of institution walls.

Modern Trends

The institution is an essential part of a total program for the mentally deficient. It provides for many who cannot be advantageously cared for in the community. By continuous study and observation, it learns the potential for community life of all who come to its doors. Most important of all, it gives the basic training that enables every patient to move forward to fuller living as his development permits.

In more recent years the development of promising new trends can be observed. One of them is that more attention is given to the personality of the patient. Many institutions now offer individual psychiatric service. As part of a more intensive treatment program, group techniques are coming into use in a number of places, as at the state schools and colonies in New York and the Brandon State School, Vermont.

Dr. Isaac N. Wolfson, when Director of Newark State School (New York) described the group treatment used there. He noted that some mental defectives have emotional and behavior abnormalities not explained by mental deficiency. They are caused by the same factors that create behavior problems in the normal person. Psychotherapy was indicated, and the shortage of personnel suggested group therapy. He summarized results of treating a small number of young female patients fairly similar as to age and I.Q. Eight of the twelve children showed improvement in behavior and attitudes. There was a shift from ego-centered to in-group behavior and finally to out-group interest, resulting apparently from the security and acceptance gained in the group situation. A more alert attitude was also noted. Dr. Wolfson advised group leaders to forget that the children are retarded and respond as they would to other children with problems.

Psychotherapy in the form of counseling has been found effective at Lakeland Village, Washington. A study reported in 1953 notes gains made by 50 boys who had the benefit of individual counseling by personnel of the Village in daily contact with them. Some of the boys had been at the institution for many years. The average mental age was eight years and nine months. At the end of the rating period, 28 percent showed marked improvement, 66 percent showed moderate improvement, and only 6 percent had shown no improvement either in behavior or social adaptation. The final results may be even better than those reported, since the majority of those in the moderate improvement group were still gaining as the program continued.

A study reported in 1955 describes the success of a social orientation course at the State Home and Training School, Wheatridge, Colorado. The course, begun three years earlier, enrolls a limited number of students with personality or behavior problems. The objective is to prepare them for happy life within the institution and for good adjustment later in the community. Substantial gains were reported in self-control, contentment, responsibility, confidence, and emotional stability.

Another kind of effort to develop maturity is found in New Hampshire. At the Laconia State School an interesting plan of self-government has been inaugurated for a limited group.

A factor that has accelerated changes is the endless problem of overcrowding. Institutions have had to comb their wards, and placement programs have been speeded up by the pressure for beds. Illinois, for example, though it had had a placement program for many years, began in 1941 an intensive effort to "depopulate" its institutions, and after training, to place them in the community under supervision of the Illinois State Department of Public Welfare.

In California the effect of intensive treatment of personality problems was demonstrated in a pilot study at the Pacific Colony at Spadra in 1950–51.[3] Serious overcrowding, as well as a belief that an institution should not be considered a permanent home for handicapped children led to a budget request for funds for a pilot study.

Unfortunately, the legislature did not grant enough for the two-year study planned. Provision was made for adding only one psychiatrist and one psychiatric social worker to the staff and the work had to be limited to a period of nine months with a follow-up of six months. The purpose was to demonstrate what can be done in successful community placement of high grade and borderline types whose chief problems are personality difficulties.

The study included only patients with I.Q.s over 40 admitted on indeterminate commitment with a diagnosis of mental deficiency. Comparable nine months' periods in 1948–49 and 1949–50 were used as controls because they represented similar conditions both in the institution and in the community. Success was defined as adequate extramural adjustment for at least six months. Failure was defined as adjustment of less than six months.

Activity centered on finding candidates for leave and preparing them for leave. Preparation included psychotherapy, psychiatric casework, and recreational and occupational therapy. Effort was directed to alleviating problems which were a specific handicap to extramural adjustment. Intensive work with relatives was aimed at obtaining wholesome acceptance of the patient's limitations by his own family.

The table below shows indefinite leaves (successes) in the study period compared with those in control periods:

Year	Indefinite Leaves	%
1948–49	55	6.7
1949–50	95	11.4
1950–51 (Study)	156	18.7

[3] Condensed with permission of authors, Dr. George Tarjan and Foley Benson.

The number of failures also increased during the study period but the net gain was appreciable.

The study yielded other interesting data. It was found that older patients, long in residence, could be prepared for leave, and that with good preparation and wise use of resources, the level of intelligence had little bearing on success. Previous delinquency, even of a serious nature, did not always prove a bar to successful reabsorption in the community. A clear relationship was shown between success on leave and good adjustment in the institution. In fact, intramural adjustment was found to be the best indicator of future leave success, and more reliable than pre-admission history. Adjustment in the institution was judged by general behavior, and success in school and in work. No patient failed on leave whose adjustment was good in all three factors.

A brief review after the study indicated benefits to the whole program of the Pacific Colony. The need for further study was shown by many unanswered questions, but the findings leave no doubt that individualized treatment resulted in a larger number of patients successfully returned to community life. The cost of adding two professional workers to the staff was less than one-third of the amount saved by the increased leaves. The intensive therapeutic program was therefore an economy.

Another analysis showed that relatively small increases in staff resulted in a disproportionate increase of leaves per staff member. The reason assigned is that much staff time is occupied in routine duties. As staff is increased, more time can be given to finding suitable patients and preparing them for release—the final goal of treatment.

A growing national trend is to admit to institutions children under five or six years of age. Young retarded children, especially if infirm, are sometimes a crushing burden in the home, but in the past institutions seldom accepted them, except in emergencies. Overcrowding and lack of infirmary beds is still the chief obstacle. There is also the consideration that children of that age need chiefly nursery care and cannot profit by the specialized services of an institution. Statistics, however, show a growing trend to admit young patients. In the period 1936–1948 total first admissions to institutions for the retarded increased slowly by less than one-third. In the same period first admissions of children under five years more than tripled. Pressure from the community has led to an increase of suitable facilities. Since 1950, admissions of young children have leveled off, perhaps because of more services at home.

Another trend is that institutions are steadily moving toward the community. The isolation that once characterized them is fast disappearing. Many instances can be cited of more service to the community. One of great interest is found at the Baldovan Institution, near Dundee, Scotland. Unable to meet the demands for admission, the Baldovan Institution set up community clinics and offered day care to selected cases. This is a great relief to families and also a means of training the mental defectives left at the institution from 10:00 to 5:30 daily. The plan is practical only in Dundee near which the institution is located. Equivalent service is planned for rural areas by forming day care centers with a nurse in charge. Out-patient clinics were intended to select urgent cases for admission, but their functions soon broadened to include diagnosis, vocational guidance, and advice to local schools, courts, and welfare agencies. The clinics represent an extension of trained medical care from the institution to the community, while the day care centers would be an extension of the nursing service.

Day care has now begun in this country. The Fernald State School has three classes for retarded children with I.Q.s of 50 or below, who do not fit into the usual special classes of the public schools. The children come for two-hour periods, five days a week. They meet in classrooms separated from the children living in the institution, to avoid the danger of introducing infections. One of the classes takes Cambridge children. The city of Cambridge transports them to the Fernald School, and pays the salary of the principal teacher. The institution provides buildings, equipment, and supporting services. The other two classes accommodate 15 children each from the neighborhood of the Fernald School. Since they come from different school systems, the institution pays the teachers from state funds. Methods for transportation vary. In some cases parents bring the children, through a car-pool arrangement; in others the school systems send them by bus.

The service has proved very popular and it is intended to develop it in other state schools. It is felt that the children have benefited, especially in self-care and group living.

The Lapeer State Home and Training School, Michigan, also has day classes. In Connecticut, the two state training schools originated day classes in rent-free rooms in Hartford and New London. The movement to provide day classes, however, has not reached substantial scope throughout the country.

The Brandon Training School, Vermont, is conducting an interesting program jointly with the Office of Vocational Rehabilitation. The latter maintains two Rehabilitation Homes in Vermont. They are supported entirely by the Vocational Rehabilitation Division. The purpose is to aid in social and vocational adjustment those who have received or are about to receive occupational training under the Division. The Training School places clients on a visit status and assumes legal responsibility besides providing personnel.

More than a century has passed since the first institution for the retarded in this country was opened in 1848. In that time the whole concept of mental deficiency has radically changed. As understanding grew, so did institutional programs. As the purpose changed from custodial care and the doors slowly opened, the institution has followed its patients into the community. The development of extramural programs is described in the following chapters.

XIII. *Colonies*

WHEN the hue and cry concerning the "menace" of the mentally deficient was at its height, there were some who had long worked with the mentally handicapped to whom it seemed inhumane as well as uneconomical to confine in an institution at considerable public expense many strong, able-bodied persons who had never committed any serious offense. These workers believed that it was both possible and desirable to remove groups of patients from the institution proper and to place them in a more normal living and working environment where they could be partly self-supporting but still remain under the necessary supervision. Not only would this benefit the patients involved, but needed beds in the institution would be released for more urgent cases.

This was the colony idea. Considerable discussion has centered around the beginnings of the colony system, largely because the term has been applied to several different types of care. The expression has been used frequently in the literature as a synonym for institutional care, and is even sometimes used in naming an institution. The word "colony" however, has come to be more properly applied to groups of patients from the parent institution who have been settled at points more or less distant from the institution but who still remain subject to its jurisdiction.

Pioneer Colonies

The first colony for the retarded on record in this country was that for retarded women established at Newark, N.Y., in 1878, as an offshoot of the institution at Syracuse. It rapidly developed into a custodial institution and in 1885 was incorporated as a separate institution. The first distinctly organized working colony established in this country, so far as the records show, was opened in 1882 on a farm at Fairmount, N.Y., by the Syracuse State School. In 1893 the Indiana School for Feebleminded Youth opened a farm colony of the same type. The colony was successful from the first and is still operating. The institution at Fort Wayne now has another farm colony.

Massachusetts followed Indiana. At the State School at Waverley, as early as 1899, Dr. Fernald, then Superintendent, became aware of the urgent need of an outlet for some of his male pupils. The excellent training had reared a group of patients capable of supporting themselves in whole or in part; yet the institution thought it unwise to discharge many of these. As Dr. Fernald explained: "We were appalled to find that, instead of a school, we were rapidly becoming a receptacle for chronic adult imbeciles, trained to the extent of their ability. There was no opportunity to exercise the trained capacity." [1] This, it must be borne in mind, was more than a decade before there was any thought of developing a parole system. It was also in the days before the "discovery of the moron" when the institution sheltered mostly lower grade types.

As a solution of this problem, the trustees purchased, sixty miles from the parent institution, a site for a farm colony for boys. The Templeton colony was the first of its kind to be operated any considerable distance from the parent institution.

The Rome Colony Plan

The colony plan had its most extensive development in New York, and to the late Dr. Charles Bernstein, then Superintendent of the Rome State School, goes the credit for having developed it in an extensive and practical way. In 1915 Dr. Bernstein wrote: "It seems the time has arrived when we must do other than make the support of the defective and dependent classes a dead load or

[1] Fernald, "The Templeton Farm Colony for the Feebleminded," *The Survey*, 27:1873.

burden on the state. Something more economical and many times more humane than brick and stone walls and iron fences may meet the need." [2] Dr. Bernstein in fact had anticipated this statement with actual demonstration and had established his first farm colony for boys in 1906 and his first domestic colony for girls in 1914.

Largely because of his work the Rome colonies have been particularly noteworthy, not only because of their variety, extent, and the large numbers of persons colonized, but also because of the application of several new principles to colony operations: (1) colonization of women as well as men; (2) establishment of industrial colonies in towns for both men and women in addition to farm colonies for men and domestic colonies for women; (3) use of the colony as a training center for community life and as a midway station between the institution and parole; and (4) the development of junior colonies.

The Rome colonies are not merely a modified form of institutional care, they are a definite part of the training for social living. The colony is one stage in the moving-up process. At the same time the Rome colonies also provide indefinite care for those "boys" and "girls" who can safely enjoy the degree of freedom which the colony affords but probably can never be entrusted to the outside world.

Colony care at Rome may be described in three phases: a development period from 1906 to about 1920; a period of great activity from about 1920 to 1935, when 60 colonies were in operation, caring for nearly 1,000 patients; a period from about 1935 to the present, when the number of colonies decreased. In this last period there was emphasis on improved sanitary facilities and comfortable surroundings under closer supervision from the institution.

These changes were not entirely due to changes of policy in the management of patients. From 1910 to 1930 there was great economic prosperity. Farm and industrial workers were in demand. In the 1930s there was industrial decline. Many houses

[2] Twenty-first Annual Report, Rome State School,

were available as well as the labor for remodeling them, and the number of colonies increased rapidly. From the late 1930s until the early 1950s other economic changes occurred. The 40-hour-work-week law for State employees went into effect. An acute housing shortage developed. During the war, when there was no new construction, old houses were in demand and the state was unable to continue renting them. The competition for labor in industry made it difficult to secure personnel to maintain colonies, and transportation problems made it hard to service them.

In the meantime new building at the institution had made some 1,500 new beds available. Chiefly because of termination of leases, children of school age were brought back to the institution where improved facilities had been provided.

Because of administrative difficulties some of the more distant colonies were transferred to other state schools closer at hand. The state purchased land adjacent to the institution. Farm colonies fifteen or more miles distant were closed and farming procedures were centralized.

In some fifty years of colony care the Rome State School has adapted its program to changing conditions, but not because of the failure of the colony plan. In January, 1957, there were some 266 patients in colonies of the Rome State School.

Despite the many changes from without and within, the Rome colonies continue to fulfill their original purpose—to train patients for community placement and to relieve overcrowding at the institution. They offer one means of overcoming the greatest drawback to increased provision for training—the high cost of institutional construction and maintenance. But the most important question is always, of course, whether the colony is desirable and successful from the standpoint of the individual and of society.

The Rome Colonies for Boys

FARM COLONIES   Consider, for example, boys in the institution who have reached the ages of twelve to fourteen or more, who are unable to make further progress in school work, but who show no special ability. Such boys may be transferred to a colony for training. The typical colony houses from 16 to 24 boys under the immediate supervision of a farmer and his wife, who have been carefully chosen and prepared for this type of work.

The first Rome colony experiment was made in 1906 when a group of 8 boys was placed on a farm about a mile from the institution. The number of boys was later increased to 20. The success of this colony led to the establishment two years later of a second, adjoining the first. Both were purchased outright.

At two-year intervals, the third and fourth farm colonies were established. Each accommodated 30 boys. A farm of 300 acres near the institution was used for raising fodder, for pasturage, and for stabling the institution's large herd of young cattle. The work was of course done by the boys. Another farm of 50 acres was devoted to truck gardening and here the boys raised practically all the vegetables needed for the large institutional population. In 1915 and 1916 two dairy farms were rented and 20 boys placed on each. These two farms produced much of the milk and butter needed for the institution. The further development of farm colonies was simply a repetition of the previous ventures. It was found generally more advantageous to rent houses and farms for colony purposes, than to purchase.

The earlier farm colonies had been, after the first year, entirely self-sustaining. With the further extension of operations, the colonies have not been entirely self-supporting. That is, while the earnings of the boys are much more than enough to pay the rent on the property, they are not sufficient to meet the entire cost of maintenance. Complete self-support had been possible in the case of the earlier farm colonies because particularly good farms had been chosen and the most capable boys had been selected to operate them.

As new farm colonies were opened, boys younger, less trained, and of lower mentality were sent out. They were not expected to be entirely self-supporting. Nevertheless their earnings covered the rent and a portion of the maintenance also. This actually

meant added accommodations at little cost to the state. Furthermore, the colony for many cases meant the difference between
life-long institutional care on the one hand and the possibility of
eventually returning to the community on the other.

As colonies have developed, more attention has been paid to
the accommodations which the farmhouse will afford than to the
condition of the farm itself. The main object is to substitute for
the inevitable routine of the institution a wholesome, normal
home environment with its small group, its family spirit, its colony mother and father, its outdoor interests, its growing things,
its live stock, and its comparative freedom. Entirely secondary
is the consideration of how good a farm a particular parcel of
land makes or even of how efficient the boys are as farmers.
Therefore the success of the farm colonies cannot be measured
in terms of economic goods produced; it can be measured only
in terms of human values. This emphasis upon the individual
rather than upon the operation characterizes the Rome colony
work.

For the retarded boy whose institutional training has been
completed but who is not yet ready to make his way in the outside world, the colony is a real opportunity. He no longer feels
like a prisoner locked up for something, he knows not what. He
finds himself in the open country, on a farm in which he feels
he has a part interest. There is much to learn but now no painful
teaching process is required. He delights to do the tasks assigned
to him, and he learns by doing. He begins to hold up his head
in the knowledge that he is working and at least helping to pay
his way in the world.

With all the freedom that the colony provides, the boys, without being overconscious of it, are still under careful supervision.
From the standpoint of segregation they are just as safe there as
in the institution. They are, besides (in nearly all the colonies),
not far from the institution. Any boy who, after fair trial, does
not like the farm life is permitted by his own choice to return to
the school. Thus there is assured in the colony a more or less like-
minded group.

In addition to the able-bodied boys who are sent out to do the farm work, two or three other boys not capable of working in the fields, sometimes crippled, are chosen to be house boys, to assist the colony mother in preparing meals, caring for the rooms, and doing light chores.

Some of the boys (over sixteen years of age) who are successfully adapting themselves to the colony life have mental ages as low as five years. From this point the mental ages range to the high grade borderline cases, the average mental age being about eight years. As regards farm work, at least, there is apparently no close correlation between mental age and working ability, some of the best workers having mental ages of seven and eight. This statement, however, must be qualified because farming, like other occupations, requires work of various kinds, some demanding more intelligence than others. For example, at Rome, boys working on crops are not considered good workers (though they may be hard workers) unless they can learn to distinguish vegetable seedlings from weeds, and to pull up only weeds. If a boy cannot learn this, farming is not for him.

The amount and kind of supervision given makes a great difference in productivity. Those with less ability need more supervision to accomplish as much as those of more ability. Even to weed a row of vegetables requires either a great deal of supervision or a fair amount of intelligence.

The boys work eight to nine hours a day. Their work is directed by the colony supervisor who is responsible to the head farmer of the institution so that the activities on all the farms are coordinated. The boys have their evenings, Saturday afternoons, and Sundays to themselves. They find their own amusements in group activities and friendships. Baseball is usually the order of the day for Saturday afternoon in summer. They may go to the institution for band concerts, motion pictures, dances, and entertainments. What they earn now and then by helping out a neighbor for a few hours they are allowed under advisement to spend. They often have enough to buy clothes. Then there are such incidentals as candy and fishing tackle. Smoking is restricted because of the fire hazard.

How do the boys themselves like this life with all its hard work and simple pleasures? I have happened in of an evening at different farm colonies. A small cluster of boys is frolicking on the lawn; several others are reading papers from home. One boy sits on the kitchen steps transplanting geraniums for the colony mother. Another boy playing with a kitten, tells you proudly in his stammering, halting voice: "A-a-aat's m-m-my c-c-aat." An animated circle of boys soon draws about ready to tell you anything about the farm and the crops. They are at home.

The boys become greatly attached to the horses, cows, chickens, and other farm animals. Many of them have their own pets, rabbits, guinea pigs, cats, and dogs. Others are permitted to have their own chickens to raise, or their own vegetable or flower gardens. All these special interests have a great stabilizing influence, especially to be noted in the case of many formerly unruly boys.

From the disciplinary standpoint the boys give less trouble in the farm colonies than in the institution. In the institution they feel more or less confined; their interests are not closely directed to anything; there is a surplus amount of energy; there is greater likelihood of friction with fellow-patients or attendants. In the farm colonies the boys like the life; they have an absorbing interest in many things; they have plenty of hard, steady work and little inclination after a full day's toil to pick quarrels or get into mischief; and they feel free. At night they are tired and after a bit of recreation are ready for a sound night's sleep.

While the conduct of many difficult boys is almost immediately transformed in response to the colony environment, others carry over their troublesome behavior into the colony life and attempt to form cliques of trouble-makers about them. Some appear to be generally unadapted to colony life. These are returned to the institution for further study, training, or discipline, as needed. If after this period, they again show possibilities of adjusting to colony life, they are given another trial, usually in a different colony. Sometimes boys are tried in five or six different colonies, with intervening periods in the institution, before they find the one in which they are able to adjust and live comfortably. Some patients do not adjust well in a group at any time. For them colony life appears unsuitable.

THE INDUSTRIAL COLONY It has been the experience of the Rome State School that farm work offers the best vocational outlet for the large majority of the males. For the minority, however, who by temperament and aptitude prefer mechanical or odd-job work and town life, the Kossuth Colony was opened in 1917 in the city of Rome. The boys were employed at various kinds of odd jobs, helping in stores, running elevators, serving as janitors, assisting painters, repairing bicycles, delivering merchandise, caring for lawns and furnaces, or shoveling snow.

The Kossuth Colony showed that satisfactory supervision can be maintained over the boys in a town colony as well as in a farm colony. The colony was favorably received by the townspeople and the services of the boys were constantly in demand. It was closed in 1946 because the house was sold by the owner and the state was unable to rent property to replace it. The industrial training it offered has been continued at the institution proper.

JUNIOR COLONIES A later development in the colony work at Rome was the establishment of junior colonies for selected boys and girls between the ages of six and fourteen. The purposes were: to get many of the teachable children away from the institutional atmosphere and to bring those of approximately the same age and mental ability together into small groups; to give these children the more normal and homelike atmosphere of the colony where, in addition to their schooling, they could learn something about home duties and home life; to supplement the school work with the practical vocational training offered by the farm and chores, and, for girls, the domestic work of the household; to prepare these boys and girls for life in the working colonies after they reached the age of fourteen or above; and finally to increase the capacity of the institution at relatively low cost. Though the junior colonies were successful for many years, they have been closed, chiefly because of termination of leases.

The Syracuse State School, in addition to several colonies for older boys and girls, maintains at Fairmount five cottages for boys of twelve to sixteen years. Each has a capacity of 40, and is used primarily for children who do not adjust well in large groups. One cottage has been set aside for the Boy Scout troop.

The usefulness of the colony plan for boys has been amply demonstrated. The colony has sometimes succeeded where the best resources of the institution have failed. It provides practical vocational training, real personality development, and the opportunity to return to community life. And to the public the colony offers a means of training large numbers of the retarded, without heavy tax burdens, and returns to society the dependable man power which the colony develops.

The Rome Colonies for Girls and Women

From the colony for boys to the colony for girls seemed to many a long and hazardous step. The Rome State School was the first, and for many years the only, institution in the country to develop colonies for girls and women, and its experience has therefore been followed with keen interest.

The colony for girls, as developed at Rome, consists of a group of from 16 to 60 girls, living together in a rented town dwelling, under the care of one or more matrons. The majority of the girls in colonies are over sixteen years of age, and are regularly employed for wages. By 1928, the Rome State School had fifteen colonies for girls in active operation; eight of the domestic service type, housing 232 working girls; three of the industrial type, housing 70 working girls; three of the junior or school type, housing 43 younger girls; and one of the custodial type, housing 22 older women too feeble to be employed. This made a total of 367 girls and women in colonies as compared with 592 females in the main institution. In 1955 there were 103 girls in colonies. As explained earlier, changing economic conditions and newer methods of care have somewhat altered the colony program, though not its purpose.

The transfer of girls from the institution to working colonies is made in no perfunctory or casual manner. Behind the entrance of a girl into colony life lies a period of careful study, training, and observation, which begins the day she enters the institution. Girls under fourteen are usually assigned to the School Department, with its habit-training classes for those with intelligence quotients below 50, and its academic work, combined with manual training, for those with more ability. Girls over fourteen (except those of quite low intelligence) are usually assigned training in the laundry, kitchens, serving rooms, dining rooms, and sewing rooms, also in general ward work and care of employee's quarters.

There is a close tie-in between the Occupational Therapy and Social Service departments. The latter has to do with the selection of girls for colonies, parole, family care, and subsequent supervision. A careful record is kept of each girl's progress in personal development and vocational ability. Consequently, when the question of promoting a girl comes up, the Social Service has an intimate knowledge of each girl on which to base its decision as to whether she has developed the personal characteristics and working ability that make her ready. If care in a colony seems indicated this knowledge also affords the means of determining to which colony she would probably be best adapted, and what kind and grade of work she could best do.

This first placement is not considered final, but rather a test which may indicate the kind of further training required. It not infrequently happens that a girl is returned several times from one or another colony to the School for further training. A girl is not looked upon as a failure on this account. It is considered a part of the adjustment process. Even when a girl comes back for disciplinary reasons, the School receives her with an understanding spirit and hopefully makes a fresh start in preparing her for another change. It often requires much forbearance and faith before a girl is enabled to find her place.

In one of the peak years, a total of 659 females were in colonies. In all, 209 colony girls were returned for shorter or longer periods, 58 of them for conduct difficulties. Of these 58 returns, however, only five were due to serious lapses.

Placement in a colony, whether a first placement or a replacement, is never made automatically, but is always a privilege to be won by good conduct and ability. It goes without saying that the matron is the one most important single factor in the success of the colony group. The matron, even with the assistants assigned her in the larger colonies, cannot make her colony successful without outside help. She needs the friendly and understanding cooperation of influential persons in the community.

Most girls placed in colonies remain there for one to four years depending on age and their response to training. The patients in the institution are eager for colony life and the possibility of promotion to a colony serves as an incentive to effort. Colony girls sometimes return to the School to visit. Well-dressed and confident, they make a deep impression.

Colony funds provide for spring and fall shopping tours, so that girls have new outfits twice a year. An allowance is given each girl for small expenses such as motion pictures and incidentals. Their wages are deposited in separate accounts at the institution, less the cost of board and room at the colony. All-round training fits them for domestic work in selected homes, to which they go back and forth alone. In groups of two or three they go to shops, movies, and church. They learn to live in an atmosphere like that of an average home.

The colony not only trains girls for work, but also guides development in other important fields. Some of the girls, because of damaging early experiences are unable to make friends. The colony may give them their first opportunity for normal human relationships. There too, they are encouraged in personal grooming and care of nice things. Recreation is considered important. Sometimes vacations with pay are arranged and many girls have attended YWCA summer camps.

DOMESTIC SERVICE COLONIES The first colony for girls established by the Rome State School was opened in 1914. It was located in a rented dwelling in a good residential section of Rome, two miles from the institution. It accommodated fourteen girls.

The girls selected for this first colony had been carefully trained for domestic service. They found employment in households that had been previously investigated and approved by a social worker from the School. Most of the girls were employed by the day and continued to live in the colony house. Other selected girls, of the more responsible type, were permitted to live at their places of employment.

During the first year 67 girls were sent to this first colony. At the end of the year 42 girls remained there or in the places of employment. Twenty-five girls were returned to the institution. The 42 girls who had made good in and through the colony showed by their demeanor and their increasing ability as workers how greatly they had benefited. The previous histories of the large majority of these girls showed a series of social failures.

During the year, the girls worked for 226 different families in the city of Rome. The housekeepers of the city quickly recognized an opportunity and the requests for the girls' services, from approved homes, were greater than could be filled.

Following the success of this first colony for girls, a second colony of the domestic service type was started two years later, also in the city of Rome. Requests for the establishment of similar colonies soon followed from responsible citizens in other towns of central and western New York.

The typical colony occupies a double frame house of inviting appearance on one of the principal streets. The interior is that of an attractive home. The comfortable furniture, the canary, the flowers here and there, all show that this is a place to be lived in and enjoyed. Upstairs, the bedrooms are papered in dainty flowered patterns, and are immaculate. Each room contains two or three beds. The bedspreads, the bureau scarves, the pictures, and other personal touches display the individual tastes of the girls.

Residents have made the girls welcome, particularly through

the churches. The girls attend the nearest church of their faith. They are held up to a high standard of behavior in the colony and are returned to the institution if signs of possible social or personal difficulty appear, and usually before serious consequences ensue. Moreover, there is the opportunity of another chance. In many cases, during this process of trying out, stabilization develops and the typical history of the girls is one of a succession of contented years of uneventful life and work.

It has been found that there is no correlation between I.Q. and misconduct, or with the number of years under supervision.

INDUSTRIAL COLONIES   World War I conditions played their part in suggesting a new industrial outlet for the girls. The textile factories were hard pressed with government orders. The Utica Knitting Mills were so anxious to get help that the company purchased a house adjacent to its plant at Oriskany Falls, which it rented to the institution at a moderate rate. This colony was opened in 1917. Twenty-four girls were placed in it and all but three or four, who were retained as house girls, went to work in the mill. The fact that this company continued to employ the colony girls after the war emergency had passed and invited the institution to establish similar colonies adjacent to its other plants at Richfield Springs and Clayville indicates how well these girls satisfied their employers.

The colony girls received the same rate of pay as other girls or women doing the same work. Wages were on a piecework basis. When economic conditions partly closed this avenue of employment, the girls found work which could be carried on in a small building on the property of the colony house. This work consisted of the handstitching of baseballs for a sporting-goods company in an adjoining city.

More recently Rome has placed girls chiefly in domestic service, though recognizing that they might succeed at other kinds of work. In domestic service the girl lives in the employer's home and is under kindly supervision at all times. Homes can be rigidly selected because of many applications.

Almost equivalent to a job in a private family is placement in a small institution. The Eastern Star Home near Rome furnishes an example. At times as many as 12 colony girls are employed there. Sometimes girls who are a little difficult to get along with in a family do well in less intimate surroundings. Regular hours, variety in work, and companionship with other girls aid in adjustment.

Girls may return to the colony if they are unhappy, and it is usually arranged to have them spend their free time either at the colony or with other girls under supervision.

The colonies described above receive all of their cases from an institution for mental defectives. A later development in some states was to accept for supervision in small units, cases direct from the community.

A Social Appraisal

Although farm work and domestice service offer many opportunities to the retarded, the colony is not restricted to any one kind of occupation. It may serve to prepare retarded youngsters for many different types of work in either city or country. It must be borne in mind that the primary objective of a colony is not vocational training in any specific field, but social training and experience, which are basic to success in all occupations.

The colony is, so to speak, the sheltering arm of the institution extended into the community. It is not a blind alley but rather a proving ground. It is an important stage in the process of developing human materials. It not only aids in further conditioning those materials but it also tests them out to determine their readiness to become once more a part of the social fabric. Entirely aside from the great service it renders in enabling the institution to extend its helping hand to a larger number of urgent cases, the colony plan is used to fill one of the great needs in the mental deficiency program—that of a safe midway station between the institution and community life.

Going hand-in-hand with the work in the colonies is the institution's parole system. In 1912, the State Charities Law relating to the Rome State School for Mental Defectives was amended to give the superintendent authority to grant a parole or leave of absence to any patient of the institution.

The parole system (in New York called convalescent care) furnishes another and further means of testing the ability and the readiness for life outside the institution. The School is the first selective agency. Certain cases need long-continued or permanent care within its walls. Others, after a more or less extensive period of training, are capable of the fuller and freer life of the colony. The colony again selects. Certain boys and girls are capable of this degree of self-support and are ready for this degree of freedom, but no more. These cases may stay in the colony indefinitely. Others, after a period of colony life, prove themselves by conduct and industry ready for the next step, a trial in the community under supervision, in family care, or on parole. Later the patient may be discharged. The discharge is not granted, however, until the authorities of the School have assured themselves that some capable person, relative, guardian, or friend, will look after him or her and give needed counsel, encouragement, and supervision.

Many of the boys in farm colonies go out from time to time for brief intervals to assist neighboring farmers. This paves the way for parole. The boy who is placed on working parole goes with all his personal belongings to make his home with the farmer year 'round. The farmer who takes him makes an agreement with the director of the institution as to wages, reports, etc.

The wages paid the boys while on working parole with a farmer vary with their ability. The wages are not paid directly to the boy but to the institution where they are deposited in a savings fund to his credit. The farmer deducts whatever has been necessary to spend for the boy's clothing and other needs, and the small amounts which have been allowed the boy for spending money. Upon discharge, the balance in the savings account is transferred in the boy's name to his local bank.

The profit the boy derives from this experience on the farm is not limited to his savings. Nor is it limited to the valuable training he receives in farming. The greatest gain to the boy is the chance afforded him to enter into normal family life, to become a member of the household, to have a personal interest taken in him. Such an experience can do vastly more than anything else in the whole program of helping him to become a socialized member of society.

How often our modern placing agencies stress the fact that limited capacity is not the chief bar to employment, but rather poor social adaptation in behavior and outlook. The colony program provides one means of meeting this paramount need, the socialization of the retarded.

XIV. *Family Care*

IN the village of Geel, Belgium, the principal occupation is the care of mental patients in family homes. This unusual service was the forerunner of family care for the retarded.

According to legend, an Irish princess, Dymphna, fleeing from her irate father, took refuge in Geel in the year 853. She was pursued by the king's soldiers and beheaded. It was said that some "lunatics" who witnessed the scene were shocked into sensibility. The cures were considered miraculous, and Dymphna became the patron saint of the mentally ill. Her tomb became a shrine and as rumors spread, hundreds of mental sufferers came to the shrine for help. There was no hospital in the small town and kind-hearted villagers took the bewildered strangers into their homes.

Whatever the truth of the legend, it is a fact that Geel has provided for the mentally ill in private homes for hundreds of years. So far as we know, this was the beginning of family care. This remarkable service has continued through the centuries and is still growing.

As time passed a hospital was established and about the middle of the nineteenth century the facilities evolved into a state colony for mental patients, now maintained as a modern treatment center with a medical director in charge. All types of mental disorders are received. Before World War II, with only a 200-bed hospital, some 3,600 mental patients were in family care. Many authorities believe that the cost of care is probably less at Geel than anywhere in the world where adequate treatment is given.

Some 500 patients are cared for at the Geel Colony each year. Indigent wards of Belgium are boarded at government expense.

Private patients pay varying rates according to the type of accommodation. Of the private rate 15 percent goes to the colony for medical service.

Careful records, subject to medical review at any time, are kept of every patient. Patients may be returned to the central institution at a moment's notice for treatment or custody. The program has been so successful that it has attracted international attention. Its success is chiefly attributed to the close supervision of patients by families and the central staff.

Many other countries have also established programs of family care. In Germany patients were placed in families as early as 1764, but at first the program was not satisfactory. Patients were not well selected and homes were not well supervised. There has since been decided improvement in the service, although war and its aftermath have interfered with progressive development.

Dr. William Griesinger, a leader in the German movement, believed that "open door" care should always be associated with the "closed door" institution. He favored both agricultural colonies and care in families. A second outstanding leader in Germany was Dr. Ernst Bufe. Besides therapeutic benefits and the facilitation of parole and discharge, he noted three practical advantages of family care: (1) it is applicable for almost all types; (2) it can be used in all countries, and in large cities; (3) it is low in cost.

When Miss Dorothea Dix visited Scotland as a tourist in 1855, she found the mental institutions very unsatisfactory. With her characteristic energy she conferred with the Home Secretary with the result that a Royal Commission was appointed to inquire into "the state of lunatics and lunatic asylums." Not only did the Commissioners advocate the building of new institutions, they also recommended the licensing of private homes, none to care for more than four patients. A supervised system of family care was authorized and an Act of Regulation passed in 1857.

France began a similar service in the department of Seine in 1890. A colony for women was established at Dun-sur-Auron in 1892, and one for men at Amay-le-Chateau in 1900. Both follow the Geel plan though on a smaller scale. Switzerland, beginning family care in 1901, soon found that it gave considerable relief to the crowded institutions. Hungary developed a colony like Geel in 1905, and later founded others, very closely affiliated with institutions. Before World War II Hungary led all countries in the percentage of patients in family care. Ontario, Canada, undertook a boarding system in 1930; and Denmark, in 1934, provided by law for placing mental defectives under supervised family care.

Family Care in the United States

Massachusetts can claim the credit for introducing family care in the United States. It was authorized for the mentally ill in 1885, and later extended to the mentally deficient. New York began family care in 1933, Nebraska in 1934, though without appropriations. Pennsylvania and Maryland followed in 1935. Some states, which have since developed similar services, met with difficulties in starting them. Utah, with permissive legislation in 1935, found that with a hospital not overcrowded, the scattered population and great distances were serious obstacles. In Minnesota, the legislature did not provide sufficient funds to pay families. The Connecticut program, first attempted in 1940, met with a shortage of social service personnel, and could not be resumed until 1949.

Family care for the mentally ill, now in practice in many states, preceded, nearly everywhere, the same service for the retarded. Thus Massachusetts, which had begun family care for the mentally ill in 1885, extended it to mental defectives about 1940. Maryland, beginning with a program at the Springfield State Hospital in 1935, developed a family care service for patients at the Rosewood Training School about 1949. California, which has used family care for mental patients since 1939, began a similar program for the retarded in 1951. In some places permissive legislation has been passed but without appropriation of funds. Despite this handicap social workers have to some extent found means of placing patients with families on an individual basis. A survey reported in January, 1956, indicated that some twenty-five institutions in the United States and two in Canada then had family care programs. Eight others planned to begin them.

In this book "family care" is defined as meaning that the state pays for the maintenance of a patient in a home not his own. In some parts of the country the term is used in a different sense. In Illinois and Maryland it describes care of patients in homes of people not related to the patient, regardless of whether board comes from relatives or other sources or whether the patient is self-supporting. The inclusion of retarded children with others in public assistance, such as Aid to Dependent Children, has the effect of providing for these children at public expense in their own homes, without their first being committed to institutions.

The first American family care program exclusively for the mentally deficient was begun in New York in 1933 by the Newark State School at near-by Walworth, a pleasant village of some 300 population about 17 miles distant. For a number of years the city of Rochester had boarded homeless children there, so that the idea of boarding homes was not new.

The Newark program, often described as an "American Geel in miniature," was begun with children of school age. In the first eight months 32 children were placed in 14 homes. Later other types of patients were placed, particularly those who required no special treatment. This policy made room in the institution for patients who could benefit by specialized training. By 1957 there were about 180 Newark patients of various types in family care.

The service was developed in other New York state schools and by January, 1958, there were 846 mental defectives in family care. As the total number in state institutions and colonies at the time was 21,493, this meant that some 4 percent of the total number were in family care.

Institutions vary greatly in their use of family care. Such differences in program may be accounted for by a number of factors —the location of the institution, the type of patient admitted, previously developed forms of care, the attitude of the director, and the availability of sufficient staff and funds.

New York has used family care longer and more extensively than other states, so that the experience there is of great interest. Two active leaders in developing the program were Dr. Horatio M. Pollock,[1] formerly statistician of the State Department of Mental Hygiene, and Miss Hester B. Crutcher,[2] for many years Director of Psychiatric Social Work of that department. For the discussion of family care the author is indebted to Miss Crutcher.

Values

So far we have discussed family care only in terms of its status at any one time or place. Of greater interest—and importance—are its advantages or values—first to the patient concerned and then to the community. It is worth noting that family care for the retarded follows the modern trend of care for other types of dependents. Normal children whose homes are broken are now boarded in private homes and the "orphan asylum" fortunately is passing from the scene. Older people are provided with public assistance or social security so that they may live in their own homes, with the family, or in boarding homes.

The benefits to the individual are many. The person is not cut off from normal activities and the opportunities and stimulation of the community. In touch with the surroundings, and having more freedom than is possible in an institution, the patient gains a greater sense of reality and is more ready to fit in and take hold of any opportunities available. Attention to individual needs draws out responsiveness. The accomplishment of small tasks gives a feeling of success, and a better personality adjustment usually results. Programs arranged by the occupational therapy department keep some patients interested, while others enjoy light housework such as ironing, cleaning silver, or raking leaves.

The obvious advantage of saving in cost should not be thought

---

[1] *Family Care of Mental Patients* (Utica State Hospital Press, 1936).
[2] *Foster Home Care for Mental Patients* (Cambridge, Harvard University Press and the Commonwealth Fund, 1944).

of as concerning only the taxpayer. The institution, relieved of a substantial number of patients, many of them custodial, can accept more cases from the community and its staff can give more time to patients needing it. The greatest saving results from less building of costly institutions with their expensive equipment.

The caretaker has the advantage of a dependable, though small, income, although homes are not selected where the money paid for the patients is the only source of income. Most patients are placed in country homes which have rooms not being used at the time. The institution virtually rents such rooms for patients, who also provide at the home table a market for produce raised on the farm. Many families welcome too, the companionship and the rewarding occupation of helping the patient.

Selection of Patients

A general rule in selecting patients for family care is that they must be harmless to themselves and others. They should also be in good physical condition so that there is no need for constant medical service. If they are able to live with relatives, or are more suited for colony life or convalescent care, they are not placed in family care.

It has been found advisable when beginning the program to place in family homes only patients who are almost certain to adjust to community living. Later more difficult types may be tried. The majority are older patients who enjoy simple home life and can care for themselves. They are selected for family placement regardless of their I.Q.s, which may range from 19 to 84, with an average of 50. Those with the higher mental levels frequently have another handicap, such as blindness or partial paralysis, which has kept them in the institution. Some of the older patients have been in the institution as long as twenty years. Even these seem to adjust well. As one superintendent has pointed out, life in a small town, with all expenses paid, makes few demands upon adaptability.

I once called at a farm home where two elderly women had been placed. It was a warm spring afternoon and both patients were sitting on the back porch peeling potatoes. The caretaker planned to take the patients that evening to a church supper, and her contribution was to be a dish of scalloped potatoes which the patients were happily preparing. They paid no attention to an old cat rubbing against them, and were so busy talking that there was some difficulty in getting answers to questions. The little picture of contentment in normal surroundings made a lasting impression.

The Newark State School furnishes a good example of success in placing both young and older children in family care. The young children are of school age with I.Q.s of 60 or more and are reasonably well adjusted. Such a "school placement" may mean that the child is entered in a special class (if there is one) in the public school. If not, he may be placed in a regular grade perhaps two years behind children of his age. The foster mother arranges for admission as if for her own children. The usual plan is to keep children in school placement until they are eighteen, when they will be transferred to a colony or employment training.

The schools accept the children without question and there are seldom difficulties. The children are not stigmatized, and are often enrolled in local Scout troops. Older children are sometimes put into family care to give them a background in family living before they are placed on convalescent care or at work. One can see how important this experience can be to a child who may never before have eaten at a decent family table, made a telephone call, written a letter, or bought candy.

Twin boys of seven were visited in the early evening. They were enrolled in a regular grade of the local public school, where they were holding their own. At the time of the visit they were struggling with their arithmetic lesson for the next day. The foster father was anxiously bending over the table trying to help them. One got the impression that the boys were bound to get on.

Dr. Charles Vaux, former Director of the Newark State School, when family care for mental defectives was pioneer work, remarked that many successes in placing children in family care do not mean that the children should never have been committed in the first place. Successes only show that when given skilled help the retarded can make good adjustments, though unaided they cannot combat such handicaps as poor home training, malnutrition and bad environment.

Selection of Homes

It will be readily seen that success of a family care program depends not only upon wise selection of patients but also on careful study of the families who will receive them. Some preparation of the community has been found advisable. The plan followed in Ohio is an illustration. A survey is first made of an area to find a desirable community. Considerations are all-year transportation, housing, recreation, education, and employment potentials. Key people are interviewed, such as physicians, clergymen (often the prospective caretaker's physician and clergyman of the patient's faith), and personnel of local welfare and health agencies. A doctor or social worker from the institution may give talks before local groups.

By the time such a survey is completed a number of possible homes will have been recommended. Other suggestions come from many sources, sometimes from institution employees or even friends of the patient. Finding suitable homes, while a complex matter, is not a major problem, because there are usually a number to choose from.

When a home has been tentatively selected the social worker makes careful inquiries and calls on the family. As well as she can, she evaluates the factors that will most affect the patient. Mature judgment is needed.

The physical standards are only those dictated by common sense. The home must provide a good bed and a place for the patient to keep things, sanitary bathing and toilet facilities, good water, and adequate diet. In some states a telephone or access to one is required, as well as reasonable protection against fire hazards.

Of first importance are the personalities of the caretaker and other members of the family. A basic necessity is security in the home, both as to family relationships and financial circumstances. A home that is ready to fall apart is not likely to be a benefit to patients. In general, younger caretakers have been found desirable for young children, and older people for adult patients. In placing children, an effort is made to avoid competition with normal children in the home. The struggles of the retarded child to hold his own may lead to unhappiness or misbehavior.

One of the considerations is to find homes that are not too different from the former surroundings of the patient. For example, patients brought up in the country do better in a village or farm home. On the other hand, city-bred patients may be frightened by the dark and quiet of a country setting. Even the change from the well-filled dormitory of an institution to a single room may cause uneasiness.

It is necessary to give the family a clear understanding of the whole situation, the limitations of the patient, the personality and background, what is required by the institution, what the state will provide. The more explicit the details of the arrangement, the less likely are misunderstandings to arise. For example, the family may be told that patients are not required to work, though they may be encouraged to do so for their own good.

Supervision

Adequate supervision from the beginning is an essential. Even when every precaution is taken, mistakes in placing are bound to occur. The sooner they are found and corrected, the better for all concerned. This means regular visits to the home by the social worker, and interviewing both patient and caretaker. The visits may be more frequent at first, but visiting once a month is considered a minimum.

Such visits are made not only to see if there are causes for complaint on either side, but also to help establish and maintain a good relationship between patient, caretaker, and institution. Practical details need discussion and there are constant adjustments to be made. If it becomes evident that even with tactful help the placement is not for the best interest of the patient, arrangements are made either for returning him to the institution or placing him in new surroundings. In case of serious illness it is usual to have the patient return to the institution for treatment.

Sometimes the program serves to educate relatives. When patients have made a good adjustment in the community, families who at first refused to take them, are willing to give them a home.

It may be the duty of the social worker to see that the patient is moved on to parole, employment, or discharge when family care has served its purpose. It should always be remembered that placement in a family is not thought of as a terminal status. Flexibility is one of the great assets of the service.

The amount of time needed for supervision is determined by so many variables that it is impractical to try to establish standards. Seldom is the social worker free of other duties so that she can give all her time to supervision. The type of patient placed, the distance between homes and from the institution, even the condition of the roads, all have a bearing. A rough estimate indicates 60 to 75 family care cases for one social worker as desirable, for the continued treatment type. For therapeutic work and young children, a case load of 40 to 50 will require the full time of one worker. Of late years community agencies have begun to share responsibility. In Rochester, for example, a family casework agency has taken over supervision of patients who have been placed in Rochester homes.

A valuable adjunct, though not a necessity, to family care is a community center for patients like that developed by the Newark State School. An arrangement was made with a nurse who had patients in care and had a house in a convenient location. Two rooms were reserved as a center for the program of the area.

One is used as a social room where patients can come and go at will. It is attractively furnished and has a radio, magazines, and games. Adjoining is another room with two beds. This is used for emergencies, or for patients remaining overnight. In cases of mild illness the nurse administers simple remedies, but a local doctor is called if needed, and is paid by the institution.

The center also serves as a depot for clothing and supplies of the occupational therapist, and as general headquarters.

Costs

The amount paid by the state to the caretaker for room, board, and laundry varies with the cost of living, the location, the type of accommodation, and the amount of care the patient requires. Thus, if the patient can take care of himself and his room and perhaps assist in the home, a lower rate is paid than if he needs constant attention. The total approximates the rate paid for boarding care of normal children.

The clothing supplied is somewhat better than that furnished in an institution. The reason is that patients must be dressed in such a way as not to be conspicuous in the community, and to be suitably prepared for all weathers and for all likely occasions, such as going to church. The original cost of such clothing is somewhat offset by the fact that at least for adults, it lasts longer. Patients take better care of nicer clothes and their wardrobes are often supplemented by gifts.

It is usual to give the patient a small allowance of spending money. This allowance is not granted if the patient is able to earn his own money.

There are items of expense, hard to evaluate, that add materially to the cost of family care. Chief of these is the expense of supervision. A social worker may include supervision of family care patients with other kinds of work, but nevertheless the time given and the cost of travel are part of the cost of the program. If the service is at all extensive, more social workers must be added to the payroll. If homes to be visited are far apart, the cost in time and travel rises. It would seem that the more cases under care the lower would be the per capita cost. Yet even this generalization must be qualified by the fact that a smaller case load, permitting more intensive work, lowers the overall expense because fewer changes in placement, hence less time, are needed.

How ever the details are worked out, it is the consensus that family care is far less expensive than institutional care.

Difficulties

The difficulties attendant upon a family care program are greater than might be expected for the administration, and less than might be expected for the community concerned. State schools for mental defectives are under different auspices in different states. In some there is a separate department of mental hygiene, in others a bureau of mental health operating under the direction of a department of health or welfare. The more divisions concerned, the more complications are involved.

How ever administered, a family care program means more work for the financial office. There is often difficulty in securing needed appropriations for staff and for adequate payment to families. There may be insufficient staff time for proper selection of patients, and in some cases there may be reluctance to release a patient who is doing useful work in the institution. A mass of detail is involved in providing for transportation, clothing, and a host of miscellaneous items. For a good family care program the whole institution must be interested, and it is no easy task to enlist the support of the many individuals and departments concerned. In some localities, housing conditions make it hard to find suitable homes; families who live in two or three rooms obviously cannot take patients. Some caretakers hesitate to take unattractive or crippled patients.

From the community point of view the story is different. Many difficulties which are expected to occur never do, and the most dreaded things seldom happen. Such opposition as may remain in the community can be diminished by educational measures. The community attitude becomes favorable as the program develops. Patients are not only welcome at churches and entertainments, in some cases admission rates are cut to fit their small allowances. There is little motivation for satisfied and happy patients to run away. Neglect and overwork are the exception and prompt action by the staff prevents these abuses from continuing. It has been found that, far from exploiting patients, caretakers tend to be too lenient. Needless to say, good management and careful supervision do much to avoid incidents. One experienced superintendent has even said, "There may be difficulties, but we cannot name them."

XV. *Community Programs*

COMMUNITY programs for the retarded call for the participation of many agencies, official and voluntary, local and regional. To be most effective, they need to be closely coordinated. This is properly a state responsibility that can best be carried out through a special service organized for this purpose.

As the whole concept of community care is constantly changing and is variously interpreted by various people, the programs, services, and ideas are as diverse as they are numerous. Colonies and their like, and family care services, such as described in the preceding chapters, are community projects in the sense that formerly institutionalized patients live and work in the community, even though such programs are directed by the state. This chapter presents only a brief high-lighting of some of the more important aspects and only a few selected outline-descriptions of the fine work that is being done for the retarded in this comparatively new and dynamic field of community care.

No state has as yet developed a community program of sufficient breadth and depth. However a number of states have developed constructive programs which, with an increased number of personnel more commensurate with the size of the problem, could constitute a satisfactory service. It would be well if legislators and others would remember, that in as far as community care overcomes the necessity of institutional commitment, this work, above and beyond its more important social results, represents a real financial saving to the state. The per capita cost of community care is trifling compared to the per capita cost of institutional care.

As an aid to the community in caring for its mentally retarded, the registration of all known mental defectives in a central state index has had many advocates. The question naturally arises, "How can we take care of them if we don't know where they are?" It is argued that the numbers must be known in order to provide needed facilities, and that cumulative records would assist all cooperating agencies. Theoretically, there is sound support for this position.

In practice, however, the desirability of registration dims as the difficulties and expense of maintenance come into view. Obviously, an index is valuable only if it is kept up to date. Births, deaths, and removals require constant revisions of the cards. But clerical work in a central office is the least of the problems. Where are the reports of changes to come from? They must come from state social workers or from local schools, health, and welfare agencies—all of which are short of staff. Few community agencies can keep up regular visits to the homes of the retarded for any length of time. Records soon become "inactive" because of pressure of more urgent work.

Most states have some form of registration. This varies from keeping an index of mental defectives who are at present or who were formerly in state schools to a real attempt to identify all mental defectives in the state and to maintain an active list. North Dakota furnishes an example of the latter. South Dakota has a list intended to include every mental defective within its borders. It is maintained by the State and is kept active by surveys and inquiries in each county.

Connecticut began a register in 1937 with financial help from the WPA. It was continued for three years, and on completion contained 28,000 names of mental defectives and epileptics. (Figures on registration must, of course, be interpreted in relation to the total population of the state concerned.) It was not possible to continue the work because of lack of staff.

Rhode Island began a register in 1942, and made a complete tabulation for the first time in 1950. The number of registered mental defectives was 6,676. The coverage was largely limited to those in the community who had become an educational or social problem, or who had been admitted to institutions.

A complete registration that would show all of the retarded in a given area appears beyond the realm of present possibility. Both state and local agencies register mental defectives who have become known to them, but all together know only a small part of the total number. It is, however, the fraction that has emerged as needing service from the much larger group of the unknown.

We may conclude, then, that the registration of mental defectives is not a prerequisite to developing services for them. Though it may be desirable, it appears that better care of already known cases is a greater need.

The Development of Parole

Parole was the first step in unlocking the doors of institutions. In mental retardation programs, the word "parole" is much less used than formerly because of its unpleasant connotation suggesting criminals and prisons. Different states use different terms such as "placement," "convalescent care," "trial visit," or "home visit." In this chapter the word is used as a convenient term meaning release, under supervision, from an institution. The extensive systems of parole maintained by almost all institutions are an important feature of community programs.

The practice of sending patients back to the community on parole was originated in 1890 by Dr. Walter E. Fernald, then Superintendent of the Waverley State School in Massachusetts. At first it was done informally. Then, in 1919, Dr. Fernald published a paper on the status of all patients who could be traced who had been released or discharged in the twenty-five-year period, 1890 to 1915. His findings showed that in general the trained mental defective was able to hold his own in the community. The next step was to legalize a system of parole, and this was done in 1922. Massachusetts' law specifically states, "No length of absence on parole . . . shall be construed as a discharge." Supervision is thus unlimited by time. The present policy is to discharge the patient when he appears able to handle his affairs reasonably well.

While other states have the same goal, practical considerations have, in some places, made it necessary to set a limit of time for parole, such as one year or two years. In some states, law, or established custom, requires that an institution be ready and able to take back any patient on parole at any time. This provision, of course, is intended to take care of failures. If the patient does not succeed on parole, the state has a place for him in the institution. Some justification for this policy is that one year is often long enough to show whether a patient can fit into the community or not. It does not mean that parole is a now-or-never procedure. One failure may only mean postponement of final release from the institution, or a trial in some other kind of supervised care. Practice in the more progressive states shows a tendency to shorten the parole period rather than to extend it indefinitely. Increasing help from community agencies favors this trend.

It cannot be overemphasized that parole everywhere is used as a step toward discharge. In New York the patient is not discharged until he has saved enough money to tide him over a period of unemployment. He must know how to find another job. Social workers help him make contact with a constructive agency, such as the YMCA. Connecticut uses a plan of trial discharge. After being on placement (parole) the patient may be given full responsibility for his own welfare for a year. If he adjusts well in this period he is granted a full discharge. Generally speaking, the patient has to show ability to get along in the community, and the parole period is adapted to meet individual needs. Some patients become self-reliant in a few months. Others need several years. Some never justify full release from supervision.

Miss Ruth A. Gegenheimer, formerly Head Social Worker at the Walter E. Fernald State School, in reviewing twenty-five years of parole service in Massachusetts (1922–1947) noted many changes both in the institution and in the community. Methods have improved. Social workers watch the patient's progress during his training and keep informed of community opportunities. As can be expected, the community is more tolerant of the retarded who are well behaved. A complicating factor is that standards for work have risen, and a state license is required for certain kinds of work, for example, hairdressing, where the retarded formerly could fit in as helpers. Miss Gegenheimer concluded that patients need as much help in their leisure time as they ever did, and that the key to success is the intelligent cooperation of the employer. Her experience indicates that the majority of well-trained and nondelinquent mental defectives of high grade can be reabsorbed into the community if adequate supervision is given.

As parole developed all over the country, institution workers found themselves in the role of job hunters. While successful employment is not the only consideration in releasing patients, it is of major importance. The mere fact that the former patient is occupied and under supervision for some eight hours a day may make the difference between success and failure. Steady work may be expected to further the stabilization of habits and personality. Ability to earn not infrequently means that patients can return to their own homes under supervision. Such considerations have led to the development of an extensive employment service which is maintained as part of the parole system in many state institutions. In Connecticut in July, 1957, there were 457 working patients living in their own homes or homes found for them, who had earned over $437,000 in one year. This is an average of nearly $1,000 for each one. It is believed that some 85 percent of the working group can later be discharged as self-supporting. Such figures speak for themselves.

But job finding is only part of the problem. Home finding is almost as important and continuous supervision may be needed until the former patient becomes established in the community. Working placements, wherein the patients live at the institution but work outside at regular jobs, are used extensively. They are especially indicated for patients who have no suitable homes.

The record of institution social workers in making successful job placements and personal adjustments for the patient is extremely creditable. Yet it would seem wise for community agencies to undertake this time-consuming service. As the resources of federal agencies become more available, part of the placement function will probably be transferred to them.

Hundreds of studies of paroled patients tell the story, of few failures, many successes. Thus the parole program, begun in 1890, without social service benefits or even the support of law, has proved its usefulness. In 1955, of 127,396 mental defectives on the books of institutions in the United States, 13,736 (more than 10 percent) were in extra-mural care other than family care.

Waiting Lists

The intense overcrowding of institutions has the unhappy result that few new cases can gain immediate admission. Names of persons for whom an application is made but who cannot be admitted are usually placed on waiting lists. If the delay in admission is brief, there may be no serious consequences, but the shortage of beds is so acute that delays in admission sometimes last months and even years. States have dealt with mounting waiting lists in various ways. A few have simply given up keeping them. Others admit only from applications or reapplications made in the preceding two years and eliminate the older ones.

Waiting lists have naturally led to careful scrutiny of applications to determine relative urgency for admission. In the course of such studies it is often found that commitment is not needed, or that another kind of care can be used to better advantage.

Connecticut long ago began a systematic study of waiting lists. In 1928, its waiting list numbered 630; in 1948, it was 667. In the twenty-year period intervening, 5,960 mental defectives and epileptics had been placed on waiting lists. Of this number, 3,301 had, at one time or another, been admitted to the training schools at Mansfield and Southbury, whose joint capacity was then about 2,700.[1]

In the period from July 1, 1938 to July 1, 1940, the number of applications placed on waiting lists was 381. In a corresponding

[1] Data are from "The Problem of the Mentally Retarded in Connecticut" by Mrs. Harriet M. Dearden, Supervisor of Social Service.

period, from 1940 to 1942, 960 applications had to be referred to waiting lists.

The Southbury Training School received its first admissions in October, 1940. With the prospect of 1,500 beds there was a deluge of applications. In later years there was a decline, for example, from July 1, 1946 to July 1, 1948, there were only 599 applications. The state now admits only from an emergency list, as vacancies occur through death or placement. In July, 1957, the joint waiting list for the Southbury and Mansfield schools stood at 860, with a prospect of 80 new beds in 1958 and 180 more about 1959.

Connecticut is by no means the only state with a serious waiting list problem. It has, however, been more active than most states in taking measures for helping the waiting applicant.

Overcrowding of institutions is a chronic problem everywhere, and as long as it persists, the necessity for the systematic study of waiting lists will continue. Undoubtedly more institution beds are needed, but the development of community facilities in the future may be expected to cut down this need for beds. Better understanding by welfare agencies of the best use of both institutional and community resources will be another factor in reducing overcrowding and its attendant evil, waiting lists.

Community Supervision

The community supervision program organized in Massachusetts deserves special mention. Massachusetts has provided traveling clinics, covering every section of the state. The program goes beyond this, however. A law enacted in 1921 provided that all court commitments of mental defectives shall be made to the Department of Mental Health, provided the commitment meets with the approval of the Department. If the commitment is accepted, it then lies in the discretion of the Department to transfer any given case to a state school or to a state institution for defective delinquents, or to allow the individual to remain in the community subject to the supervision and control of the Department, or to discharge him entirely. Psychiatric social workers on the staff investigate all cases referred for commitment, and organize services for those who remain in the community. In this way, provision is made for placing under state care a large number of mental defectives who, because of limited accommodations, cannot be immediately admitted to institutions, and still another large group of cases needing supervision but not requiring institutional care. Before this type of supervision was adopted in Massachusetts, the presence in the community of large numbers of retarded persons on institution waiting lists for months and years constituted a troublesome problem for local public officials and social workers.

This legal provision for the establishment of a minor guardianship, as Dr. Fernald called it, furnishing as it does a lesser degree of control than the institution, but control nevertheless, constitutes a very important addition to the mental deficiency program. It gives community supervision, with respect to the cases so "committed," a definite legal status. By subjecting all applications for admission to the painstaking scrutiny of a central organization, this plan also has the advantage of giving to the institutions unprejudiced reports by trained observers as to the urgency of the admission of particular cases. As a result of the investigations and adjustments made by the social workers, it has been found that the necessity of commitment can be obviated in many cases, thus reducing state expenditures and reserving institutional facilities for the more urgent cases.

A somewhat similar program has been carried out in Connecticut since 1923. Every application for admission to an institution is investigated by means of a home visit, at which time a complete history is obtained, and the social and economic conditions of the family ascertained.

About 1930 Connecticut began a pre-commitment service to supervise at home as many waiting applicants as possible. Later social workers were assigned exclusively to the investigation of waiting lists. They attempt to call on each family at least three times a year. The list is thus kept up to date and if necessary families are helped to make other plans while waiting for the child to be admitted. The workers have also helped to organize parent groups to assist parents in caring for their children.

Since 1923, Pennsylvania has also included in its community supervision program the investigation and overseeing of those on waiting lists of state institutions. There the Bureau of Mental Health organizes the program throughout the state. Field agents have been able to render valuable service to many communities throughout Pennsylvania by stimulating and directing the organization of facilities for the study and care of troublesome cases.

In New Jersey, community care of the retarded is promoted and coordinated through the Department of Institutions and Agencies. The division of classification of this Department is used by public officials and social workers in all parts of the state as a clearing house for information concerning mental defectives in the community, and their proper care and treatment. The Children's Bureau of the Department provides a consultation service for the welfare of problem children, including the retarded. Examining service is available to the communities of the state through clinics conducted by the Department.

Minnesota has an outstanding program. This state has had a guardianship law since 1917, which, through several administrative changes, serves as the basis for a flexible and comprehensive system. The Director of Public Institutions, also in charge of state schools may by law be made the guardian of any mental defective or epileptic, wherever he may be. The Bureau for the Mentally Deficient and Epileptic, as his representative, administers a service which is integrated with other state units and reaches into every community. County welfare boards are legally charged with responsibility for mental defectives and epileptics in their counties, who, when found, may be committed, not to an institution, but to the guardianship of the state. Local welfare boards, often with advice from the Bureau, plan for the best disposition of each case, whether the patient requires supervision at home, boarding care, or institutionalization.

Guardianship is continuous and a ward may be transferred from one kind of care to another, as seems desirable. The ward may also be discharged from care when supervision no longer seems necessary. Not all of the retarded known to authorities are committed to guardianship, but they may be so at any time—through appropriate court action. Thus the rights of the individual are protected.

Besides the obvious merits of flexibility and wide coverage, the system has the very great advantage of uniformity in policy. The state furnishes a manual to county welfare boards, which clearly sets forth policy, pertinent laws, procedure, and duties. In addition the Bureau works closely with welfare boards, and must be notified before commitment to guardianship is initiated. The state thus controls admission to institutions, can classify applications, and establish waiting lists in accordance with needs. A further advantage of the program lies in the fact that primary responsibility rests on agencies in the community where most mental defectives actually live. There is also the added value that welfare agencies give service to the retarded as part of general casework and thus do not single them out as a separate class.

In New York a bill was passed in 1958 to establish a community center in the western part of the state. The center will provide services for retarded adults and all retarded children not in institutions nor public school classes. The program will include day training centers, recreation, sheltered workshop and vocational guidance for adults, counsel for parents, and a residential half-way house for those entering or leaving institutions. The community supervision programs must be operated hand-in-hand with the institution, the public school, the courts, and other public and private agencies that are dealing with the problems of retardation.

Clinics

The growth of clinics has advanced care of the retarded, although it has not been on a scale at all commensurate with needs.

About 1920, a few states organized clinics to identify and serve mental defectives in the community. The clinic systems of several states have been mentioned earlier.

New York began a clinic service in 1919, when four field agents were appointed by the former State Commission for Mental Defectives, later absorbed by the State Department of Mental Hygiene. The clinics were thinly scattered in population centers throughout the state, and were held in quarters available without rent, such as schools and health offices. In the early years psychiatrists were borrowed from near-by state schools or other institutions.

The clinics were at first intended for mental defectives only, but it was soon found that there was urgent need to include children with other problems. The clinics, therefore, were broadened to a child guidance service. They were a boon to welfare agencies which had had no previous help. Just how welcome they were was dramatized once while the Commission was arranging a date for a rural county. It received a telegram pleading, "We want the clinic even if you have to visit us in the middle of the night."

The staff was soon increased and the whole system has steadily developed. Full-time teams now operate in regions of a few counties each, an arrangement which, by cutting down time spent in travel, permits more concentrated work. The policy is to give service in rural and semirural areas, as large cities can provide for themselves at least part of the service needed.

Most of these clinics now emphasize the treatment of all children, including the retarded, with personality, behavior, and habit disorders. Referrals of children whose problem is purely educational are no longer accepted. Responsibility for diagnosis of retardation has been shifted as far as possible to school systems, with a confirming opinion required from the state's education department.

Child guidance clinics were gradually established throughout the country. These clinics treat various types of mental health problems of children. Retarded children may attend many of them, but there are clinics that do not accept retarded children even for diagnosis.

Although the number of child guidance clinics has sharply increased since about 1946, the mental health clinic service for children is woefully inadequate. The relatively few clinics open to retarded children provide mostly for diagnosis only. Rare indeed are supporting services, such as the treatment of remediable physical defects, faulty speech, and personality disorders, or the giving of professional advice to parents. However, signs of progress are appearing. For example, public funds are granted for the support of clinics of large scope like the special clinic at the Flower-Fifth Avenue Hospital of New York City.[2] Substantial funds have now been appropriated for new clinics for the retarded in many states. An important feature of clinics is that provision is made for the training of personnel.

Consultation with parents may need emphasis. Since the vast majority of the retarded live in their own homes, obviously most of the responsibility for training falls upon parents. Skilled and sympathetic counseling at the time of the first diagnosis of deficiency is of supreme importance. To plan and carry out a program for the child's fullest development parents must have a clear understanding of his limitations and future possibilities. Each child and each family is different. To be of any value, discussion must center on the individual child in his own family and neighborhood.

Clinics, an indispensable part of a program for the retarded, have so far, in the country as a whole, served only a scanty few. There are only some seventy clinics specialized for the retarded. In the future we may expect clinics to be not only more numerous but also more useful, in that they will serve the whole child and the family that rears him.

[2] See *American Journal of Mental Deficiency* (July, 1957), "The Relationship of the Flower-Fifth Avenue Hospital Clinic for Mentally Retarded Children to a Community Wide Program in an Urban Setting," by Smith, Giannini and Slobody.

Local Agencies

The extension of state services to the community is one of the most valuable elements in a comprehensive program for the retarded. State mental health authorities are slowly accepting more responsibility for those mental defectives not in institutions. This is shown not only in extra-institutional service but by the appointment in a number of states of special commissions to study the needs of the retarded.

Closer cooperation with local agencies is another favorable development. Neither the state nor the community can assume the entire burden, and harmonious cooperation offers the only hope of a really sound program.

The success of a social rehabilitation program that is geared as it should be to life planning depends upon a close working relationship between community agencies and the institution. Colony, family care, and parole programs are so much an integral part of the institution's training program that the administration of these activities should remain a function of the institution. It is only when the institution has relinquished responsibility for the individual by granting discharge that the community should render active service as needed. Although discharge presumes the ability of the individual to get along satisfactorily in the community, it usually does not mean that there should not be at least a modicum of friendly supervision. Before a case is discharged, the social worker of the institution seeks to provide for such oversight through responsible relatives, employers, or welfare agencies. But after a short time, the institution is no longer able to keep in active touch with most of its discharged cases, and unless there is organized community supervision to assume responsibility at this point, these cases are apt to be left to themselves for better or for worse.

The follow-up of discharged cases offers a most favorable opportunity for productive work at a relatively small outlay of effort, comparable with that of following up the mentally deficient boys and girls leaving the public schools. Those granted discharge by the institution are, for the most part, a selected, well-trained group. They are promising material for community life.

Organized social agencies are an important point of contact for the community program. Nowhere are the ugly aspects of neglected mental retardation more glaringly revealed than in the day's work of family and child welfare agencies in both urban and rural districts. Children's agents, in responding to appeals for help in behalf of dependent or abused children, have from time to time discovered in isolated sections whole families and groups of families of the hovel type of mental deficiency, where the wretchedness and filth of the home, and the condition of the children, beggar description.

The community problems of retardation as seen by the large urban welfare agency have been the subject of many articles. Dealing as such agencies do with the social needs of the community, it is to be expected that many of the most complicated and difficult problems would come their way. A large number of mentally deficient persons in the community, however, manage to find employment, pay their bills, and keep out of difficulty. These seek no social agency, and live and die without benefit of social worker.

Facts stress the importance of building up what is now the least developed aspect of mental deficiency work, namely, community service. As experts in dealing with personal and social problems, social workers should be able to render the utmost assistance to the community in straightening out the snarls in family life which the retarded, who have been forgotten until they get into trouble, frequently cause.

Home Teaching

Several states have brought service directly into the home. Massachusetts began a home teaching program in 1940. Social workers of the Department of Mental Health visited homes to help the mother plan and carry out a simple educational program.

Later this service was superceded by the establishment of centers for young or severely retarded children in different communities.

New Jersey undertook the same kind of program in 1943, but the home teachers were trained in education rather than in social work. The service was begun as an aid to parents whose children were on waiting lists for admission to institutions. For the severely retarded, emphasis was placed on habit training, emotional control, self-help, speech, and play. Practice in simple household skills was used to develop a sense of responsibility. The classes showed that many severely retarded children can, with proper training, make a good adjustment at home, and remain there indefinitely. More recently the program has been directed to older children.

In Pennsylvania a different procedure is proving successful. In 1952 the Montgomery County chapter of the Pennsylvania Association for Retarded Children made a contract with the local Visiting Nurse Association to provide regular help in home training.[3] Within a few years a number of units in Montgomery and other counties were taking part in the program. The parents group pays for each visit. Services of the nurse include helping parents to accept the condition of the child, arranging for mental and physical examinations, training in habits of hygiene and social behavior, and informing parents of available local resources.

An important part of these programs is their contribution to the morale of the mother. Visited once a month or oftener by someone close to her problem, she no longer feels that she is struggling alone. Often the home teacher, knowing resources as she does, can help the mother take advantage of free services in the community. Sometimes the mother can be put in touch with other retarded children so that her child has companionship.

Another value of the service is that it reaches a class for whom almost nothing has been done—namely the young retarded child with a good home. Such children, who may be too young or too handicapped for acceptance in school, may still not require institutional care.

[3] Pines and Capa, *Retarded Children Can Be Helped.*

Schools

The whole subject of the public schools and what they are able and should be expected to do for the retarded is such an important one that it is given a separate chapter. What the community can do, however, in cooperation with the schools, is deserving of a few remarks here.

For retarded children in the school enrollment, the school itself should assume the entire responsibility for supervision through its social service. Practically speaking, however, and excepting the larger cities, the schools will probably not have, in the near future, enough social service to deal effectively with the extra-school problems of mentally deficient children. In these circumstances, other agencies should help to solve, or better yet, forestall many of the personality, home, and neighborhood problems of the retarded school child. This is done in some places through consultation with state services. In states having a program that covers each county, referrals can be made to local boards. Even in school systems where special classes are provided, many of the lower grade children will be excluded from school. Since few schools assume responsibility for such cases, the community agencies must be prepared to aid this group.

There is perhaps no more vital service that can be rendered by the community than assisting mentally deficient boys and girls as they leave school to make their way in the world. Even where special classes and social service are well organized, the schools have not undertaken to follow up the graduates of special classes for more than a short time. Active follow-up work seldom goes beyond aid in securing the first job. It is inconceivable that any school system would ever be able to follow up these former pupils for more than a year or two.

The community agencies should take up responsibility where the school drops it, and be ready to aid the boy or girl until such time as an apparently stable adjustment in community life has been made. There is no more important task in the whole mental deficiency program than to conserve the good results of the special training which the modern school provides for the mentally handicapped boy or girl.

The Courts

The community program should also be closely related to the courts, and particularly children's courts. It has been the custom of many courts to regard institutional commitment as the only practicable recourse in the case of children coming before them who are found to have intelligence quotients of less than 70. This policy tends to force upon already overcrowded institutions many mental defectives who do not really need institutional care, and whose removal from community life is not justified.

A specific instance of the possibilities of contact with the courts was afforded by the demonstration carried out many years ago in connection with the Juvenile Court of Cook County, Illinois.[4] The Illinois Institute for Juvenile Research had provided psychiatric service for all children coming before this court for whom petitions alleging deficiency had been filed. Such petitions had been filed on two-thirds of the cases with intelligence quotients below 70. As a result of investigations made by the Institute's staff into the intelligence and personality of the child, his home and social backgrounds, etc., the court saw fit during the four years after this special work was begun, to recommend 36 percent of the more than 1,000 children for community supervision rather than institutional commitment. Only 14 percent had been recommended for community supervision during the preceding four years.

Many retarded children are brought to court through no fault of their own, but because of neglect or improper guardianship. Even these, however, show the effect of poor home conditions and are in need of help. Few courts, except in large cities, have psychiatric service but in many places local clinics can be uti-

---

[4] Phyllis Bartelme and Paul L. Schroeder, "A Mental Health Program As a Juvenile Court Method of Supervising the Feebleminded," *Journal of Psycho-Asthenics*, 33:37–58.

lized and will arrange with the probation officer for following up children not committed to institutions.

As with the schools, court supervision does not continue long. Here is another gap in the program. Who is going to take over where the probation officer leaves off? The answer, in states that do not provide continuous supervision, must be the community welfare agency.

Federal Programs

The National Mental Health Act of 1946 established, under the United States Public Health Service, the National Institute of Mental Health. This Institute makes grants for research, for demonstrations, for training of professional personnel, and for development of community mental health services.

In addition to the program of grants, the National Institute of Mental Health conducts research of its own, makes surveys, provides consultation service on request, and stimulates development of educational programs. The Publications and Reports Section publishes a mental health film guide, reference guides, and distributes mental health educational materials. The NIMH Biometrics Branch issues periodical reports on the institutionalized mentally ill and mentally defective, and on mental health clinics.

Grants-in-aid are made through state mental health authorities. Communities seeking funds to develop local services must submit plans and requests to their own state mental health authority.

With regard to mental retardation primary efforts are focused on spurring research and program activities in collaboration with major national organizations in the field. In the fiscal year 1956 substantial initial grants were made to the National Association for Retarded Children and to the American Association on Mental Deficiency for research, for training of personnel, and for program planning in an attempt to bring together from hundreds of sources all available information in the area. Congress later greatly increased the appropriations to the National Institute of Mental Health and the National Institute of Neurological Diseases and Blindness. The latter has embarked on a very extensive study of cerebral palsy, mental retardation, and epilepsy. In a pre-natal survey some fourteen medical schools are studying a sample of 40,000 pregnant women. The children will be followed up for their first years with the expectation that. new light will be thrown on causes and treatment.

Other branches of government have also undertaken programs for the retarded. The Children's Bureau in 1954 made available $1,300,000 to health departments in thirty-one states and territories, for special demonstration projects to continue for five years. These provide for establishing clinics for diagnosis, follow-up service, and counseling of parents, with emphasis on young severely retarded children. The Children's Bureau was also granted $10,000,000 for 1957–58 and $11,000,000 for 1958–59 for strengthening state and local child welfare programs. These funds, in part, are for training personnel and for services to the retarded, heavily represented in caseloads of child welfare workers.

The Office of Education has sponsored fifty research projects in the field of retardation to study communication problems, learning, teaching methods, school organization.

Another type of government interest was shown when the Social Security law was changed in 1956. Previously, aid to a disabled dependent of an insured person ceased when the dependent became eighteen years of age. This aid (which includes the retarded) will now be continued for life.

In most states and many cities, voluntary associations maintain active programs for development of mental health resources and education.

The movement was first organized in 1908 by the late Clifford Beers, who, while a patient in a private mental hospital, was shocked to find how poor the facilities were. On recovering, Mr. Beers organized the Connecticut Committee for Mental Hygiene, with the purpose of improving services for mental patients. In the next year, 1909, the National Committee for Mental Hygiene was organized. Under its present name, the National Association for Mental Health, the Association conducts and supports research, gives leadership to affiliated state-wide and local associations, sponsors the improvement of facilities and training of personnel, and provides educational material of many kinds.

In 1910, the State Charities Aid Association appointed the New York State Committee on Mental Hygiene, now known as the New York State Society for Mental Health. As long ago as 1890 the State Charities Aid Association had a "Sub-Committee on the Feebleminded," indicating that mental deficiency has been a citizen concern for many decades. Other states organized similar groups in steady succession and the movement is still growing.

Most of these societies have adopted broad programs and have carried out a great variety of special projects. Among other concerns are some services for the mentally deficient. Their programs may take the form of assisting to pass legislation for better state facilities, making surveys, providing information, or stimulating development of local resources such as clinics or special classes.

NATIONAL ASSOCIATION FOR RETARDED CHILDREN The parents of retarded children are contributing greatly to the advancement of a modern program. Beginning about 1930 small groups of parents in different localities banded together to help each other. Organization has spread rapidly from state to state, and similar movements have developed in Canada, England and other countries.

The National Association for Retarded Children was organized in 1950. Membership grows steadily and in 1958 numbered over 60,000 and included not only parents but professional workers and interested citizens. A national headquarters with a well-qualified staff was opened in New York City in January, 1954. Some 600 state and local units cover the country. Their purpose is to help retarded children wherever they are, in home, school, or institution, and regardless of race, creed or color. Members take an active part in planning. A broad program has been adopted which includes legislation for extending public services, advancement of research, training of personnel, education of parents, development of diagnostic and treatment clinics, home training, nursery schools, increase of special classes, sheltered workshops, and improvement of institutions.

Local units of the organization are filling gaps not covered by public agencies. In many places where schools have no classes for severely retarded children, parents have established classes of their own, providing teachers, equipment, and transportation.

The shortage of qualified personnel for all phases of work with the retarded is a major concern of the Association. It constantly encourages students of medicine, nursing, social work, and teaching to prepare themselves to deal effectively with problems of the retarded they will surely meet. Recruiting teachers is another project carried out in many parts of the country. Some parent groups offer university scholarships for special teacher training; others offer bonuses to teachers already qualified. Professional conferences of many kinds are frequently arranged.

Parent organizations, by 1957, had opened sixty-seven sheltered workshops where retarded young people can learn to earn. Twice this number are in the planning stage. Hundreds of classes have been arranged to help parents understand their retarded children and aid the growth of wholesome personality. Recreation is not forgotten. Playgrounds, swimming pools, summer camps, and social gatherings are sponsored everywhere by parents who realize that learning to get along with other youngsters is a vital factor in happy, successful living.

The Association has been notably successful in stimulating public agencies to expand programs for the retarded. Voluntary groups have also become interested, for example the American Legion Child Welfare Foundation. The powerful influence of the National Association for Retarded Children is more effective every year.

Coordination of Services

The array of services described would, at first glance, seem sufficient to meet all reasonable needs. Analysis, however, shows that there are very serious weaknesses in the present program. Perhaps the most obvious is the unevenness of distribution of facilities. Some communities have a variety of services, others have practically none. Such discrepancies are found from state to state and from city to country.

Just as disastrous is the fact that nowhere are services sufficient in quantity. That they differ also in quality from excellent to substandard has already been pointed out. The fact that resources are scattered, scanty, and uneven makes it imperative to use them wisely. Coordination is the prime consideration.

The difficulties in the way of better coordination are great. The resources exist under different auspices and draw funds from different sources. They developed at different times and places. Special classes are maintained by local schools, but are supervised by a state education department. A different department controls state institutions. Social service in the community is given both by state and local workers. Some of the latter are under city or county departments supervised by a state welfare department and are financed with tax-payers' money. Others are private agencies, supported by contributions. They have to conform only to policies set by their boards, as long as they comply with state law.

In this confusion of auspices it is understandable that there are gaps in functions. In spite of obstacles, however, substantial progress toward better planning has been made and appears to be growing. We see state clinics giving service to local schools and the schools assisting federal employment agencies, the private agency working with the public. All this is in the right direction but on too small a scale.

One barrier to coordination is lack of agreement on policy, and this is a matter for the serious consideration of every person and agency dealing with the retarded. In a later chapter suggestions are made for bringing about more uniformity of thought on the basic elements of a large-scale plan.

XVI. *The Challenge to the Schools*

OF all community resources for retarded children, the public schools are of outstanding importance. Compulsory attendance laws give them, to begin with, a unique opportunity for identifying the retarded as soon as they reach school age.

The schools, in the past, had long been laboring under the heavy burden of laggard children—the bane of teachers and a drag on the progress of other pupils. Financially, it has been estimated that some 10 percent of public school expenditures in this country had gone into the waste motion of permitting over-age children to repeat grades. Modern psychology finally showed that many of these retarded children were not merely slow, or indifferent, but were lacking in the intellectual capacity for regular class-room work.

Once the public schools became aware that retarded children were present in large numbers and that simply relegating all such cases to institutions was out of the question, educators turned their attention to the organization of special classes or special schools for these handicapped pupils. This expedient, far from doing violence to educational practice, only hastened recognition of the varying capacities and differing abilities of all the children in the schools and the consequent abandonment in the more forward-looking systems of the one-for-all curriculum based on the fiction of the average child. In keeping with this modern tendency of adapting the school to the child, the special classes, at first frankly an expedient to rid the school of an overwhelming burden, are now recognized to have a rightful place in the educational system.

Thus it has come to pass that by far the largest and most important part of the whole mental deficiency program has fallen squarely upon the public schools. Although educational authorities, even in the more progressive centers, are as yet far from having made complete provision for all retarded children of school age in the community, the responsibility of the school for educating the subnormal child is now generally accepted, and appreciable progress in the organization of special classes is being made each year.

How many retarded children are to be found in the typical school system? Most authorities agree that about 2 percent of the elementary school enrollment are so mentally retarded as to require instruction in special classes. In addition to the children with quite definite retardation, there are many children in every school system who are of borderline intelligence, with I.Q.s between 70 and 90 for the most part, and others who, for the time being, are pedagogically retarded. A number of school systems have found it advantageous to organize a series of classes half way between the regular grades and the special classes. Many pupils from these classes can eventually be restored to regular grade work; a few on further observation will need to be transferred to special classes.

The special classes, by whatever name they may be called in particular school systems, are usually reserved for pupils with I.Q.s under 70 or 75. Usually excluded are children who are unmanageable in the classroom, and those who cannot attend to personal wants. Practice varies as to the lower limit of mental age for admission to special classes. At best, such classifications are only rough guides. It is no longer considered advisable to place a child on the basis of the I.Q. alone, without an individual study of other characteristics. It may be said, however, that the I.Q. and mental age are better guides for planning school work than for other purposes.

School policies are steadily broadening. A substantial number of cities have established special classes for children with I.Q.s as low as 30, or even less. Classes for severely retarded children began to appear at the turn of the century. Until the 1950s they developed slowly and on a limited scale in only a few large cities.

For practical purposes a distinction is made between "trainable" and "educable" children. The latter fit into the usual special classes and can profit from a differentiated academic education. The trainable group is usually defined to include children with I.Q.s between 30 and 50. For this group the school program is directed toward the formation of good habits for daily living and socialization.[1]

This trend toward opening the school doors to the more severely handicapped is gaining ground, in some places with the aid of legislation, in others subsidized by parents and welfare or mental health agencies. The number of severely retarded children enrolled in public schools is, however, only a fraction of the estimated number who could benefit by attending. In 1957 Dr. I. L. Goldberg, in a survey for the National Association for Retarded Children, found nearly 10,000 in public school classes. Dr. Samuel A. Kirk estimates that any community with 10,000 children from seven to eighteen years of age will find eight to twelve children suitable for special classes for the trainable.[2]

Another development has been recognition of the needs of mentally deficient children with other disabilities, such as auditory, visual, or other physical defects. Retarded children with epilepsy are usually accepted in schools if they are not a danger to themselves or others. Fouracre and Thiel call attention to the educational needs of children with cerebral palsy accompanied by mental retardation. When the school program is modified for them it is usually the physical impairment, not mental retardation, that is considered. Regardless of mental ability, they are usually placed with crippled children because of their special requirements as to transportation, stairs, toileting, or feeding. A better plan might be to group children with physical handicaps with children not physically handicapped, segregating them only to receive therapy. Those with mental retardation could well be grouped with children of similar mental and social age.

Other recourses would be structural changes in school buildings and orientation of teachers of exceptional children in proce-

[1] G. Orville Johnson, *Training Program for the Severely Retarded* (New York State Interdepartmental Health Resources Board, 1958).
[2] Kirk, *Public School Provisions for the Severely Retarded* (New York State Interdepartmental Mental Health Resources Board, 1957).

dures needed by children with both physical and mental handicaps. Such changes in school services might be expected to help children with these double disabilities avoid the social maladjustment which later may prove a great obstacle in employment, as well as a barrier to happy living.

Special classes for problem children antedated those specifically intended for the retarded. New York City and Cleveland pioneered in the establishment of classes of the former type in the '70s. In 1894, a separate school for problem children was organized in Providence from which there developed in 1896 a special class to meet the needs of the retarded children found in the problem group. This Providence class was apparently the first special class for mentally deficient children as such to be organized in the school systems of the country. Although the dates of establishment and character of the special classes are in some instances uncertain, Springfield seems to have followed Providence with a special class in 1897, Chicago in 1898, Boston in 1899, New York and Philadelphia in 1901, Los Angeles in 1902, and thereafter in rather rapid sequence, most of the larger cities of the country.

State Action

Many states have enacted statutes making mandatory or permissive the establishment of special classes or schools for mentally handicapped children in the public schools. The states that took early action were: New Jersey, 1911; Minnesota, 1915; Illinois, New York, and Wisconsin, 1917; Massachusetts, Missouri, Pennsylvania, and Wyoming, 1919; California, Connecticut, and Utah, 1921. In 1955 Dr. G. Orville Johnson made a study of educational provisions for the severely retarded. Forty-seven states replied to the questionnaire. Of these 25 had legislation concerning special classes, but 23 of them had permissive legislation only. The amount of state interest varies. Some states authorize special classes but do nothing to stimulate or finance them. Others help meet costs. Still others not only help with costs but also provide consultation, supervision, and transportation. Some of the states with the most extensive programs act with only permissive legislation, but have some stable plan of reimbursement. The most frequently found status is permissive legislation with stimulation by the state. Mandatory laws are not always successful. In one state a mandatory law became inoperative a few years after it was enacted because of lack of funds. In another, a mandatory law could not be enforced, although funds were available, because personnel could not be found.

The amount of state aid varies as much as do the laws. It may be a flat sum, as when a program is not fully stabilized. The state may pay the excess cost of special education up to a stipulated ceiling, or it may pay the whole cost, even including transportation of the children. New laws, or amendments, are constantly being passed to expand provision for exceptional children.

Legislation and state aid give great impetus to the growth of special classes, but even in progressive states nothing like a complete program of special classes has as yet been organized.

New York has had mandatory legislation since 1917, but the State Education Department estimated that in 1954-55 only about one-third of the retarded children were enrolled in special classes. More than half of the state population is in New York City, but this city had more than twice as many special classes as were found upstate. There were relatively few classes in the smaller towns. If such figures are found in prosperous New York, it is easy to guess what the status is in other parts of the country. Estimates are that from one-third to one-half of retarded children are not accommodated in special classes. In round numbers a special class is needed in any school system having 750 children in elementary grades. Fifteen children of this enrollment (using the 2 percent estimate) will be found retarded, and this number justifies establishing a special class.

The exemption of children from school attendance because of severe mental handicaps is also controlled by legislation. Although most state laws grant authority to local school boards to exclude children, the stipulation is made that the decision must be based on the certification of a specified authority, such as a psychological or psychiatric specialist.

The number of retarded children not attending school is all too easily underestimated. In New Jersey during 1951, the Department of Education attempted to compile a list of the names and addresses of all children not in school because of mental handicap. A total of 1,423 children between the ages of 6 and 16 were listed. It was believed, however, that there were actually some 2,500 children (one-third of 1 percent of the school population) for whom the state provided no education in their home communities. Similar inquiries in other states would undoubtedly reveal the same or worse conditions.

It must be noted that not all children get the benefit of laws intended to protect them from being excluded from school. It is not unusual, especially in rural and semirural districts, to find children who have been excluded by action of a local board, without legal sanction. For a retarded child to be deprived of education, or even the chance of education, is a disaster of such magnitude that the results can hardly be foreseen.

The position of the public school in the mental retardation program is unique. No other agency can begin to make so effective a contribution to the welfare of the retarded. If the public school shirks this task it is not only clogging its own machinery, but is doing the worst thing possible for these handicapped children. Such a system means for the retarded child that he soon reaches a point beyond which he can go no further. It means shame and discouragement in being left behind with younger pupils. It means loss of interest in, even rebellion against, school work. It means every incentive to truancy with its ready concomitant of delinquency. It means putting in wasted years, only to have the boy or girl drop out of school as soon as the working age is reached, without proper training with which to face the world, and with an overwhelming sense of personal inferiority. In brief, such a policy may be expected to make social outcasts of the retarded.

On the other hand, the public school which makes an honest

endeavor to do justice to its mentally handicapped children can render incalculable service. There are first the unrivaled facilities of the school, as the one agency which is in touch with all the children of the nation, for identifying the retarded.

By means of the compulsory attendance laws, the school can bring under observation every child in the community as he reaches the age of six or seven. If, by means of kindergarten attendance, clinics, and other agencies, mental retardation can be detected in the pre-school period and suitable training measures instituted, a great deal can be gained. The importance of pushing further and further back toward infancy the time when retardation is discovered and appropriate training undertaken is now generally recognized. If the public school accepts its full responsibility, no retarded child should get beyond the age of seven undetected.

Identification having been made, the next duty of the school is that of individual study and classification of all mentally handicapped pupils. This study goes well beyond intelligence tests and includes tests of aptitudes, special abilities, and disabilities, as well as a general personality study. There should be available to the school for this purpose competent psychological and psychiatric service.

The task of selection follows. While most of those studied will presumably be recommended for special or ungraded classes, doubtless some cases will be found for whom institutional care is indicated. Through study and selection on the part of the public school, mental defectives with marked antisocial proclivities can be found and treated before trouble occurs. The progressive school is a constructive agency. Of course it cannot prevent mental deficiency, but it certainly can prevent the serious consequences that frequently result from neglected mental deficiency. The public school receives the retarded while there is still every opportunity to mold personality in the right direction, and to develop limited capacities to the utmost. One needs only to consult the case records of a modern child guidance clinic to understand how much of personal and social adjustment can be done by the school which has a social point of view and has available adequate psychiatric, psychological and social service.

The school that merely concerns itself with its mentally handicapped pupils during school hours is closing its eyes to the larger part of its task. Every devoted special class teacher becomes quickly aware of the importance of following the mentally handicapped child into the home and community, and of bringing all possible forces to bear to correct conditions which tend to counteract the work the school is doing in developing the boy or girl into a social and economic asset. Many special class teachers give unsparingly of their own free time to home visiting and the organization of wholesome associations for their pupils. While it is important that the special class teacher should personally make some of these outside contacts, the burden should not fall entirely upon her. Many school systems have an organized social service on which the special class teacher can call for assistance with these out-of-school problems.

Experience indicates the amount of social service required. Of the total school enrollment one social worker is needed for every 2,000 children, or if working in a psychiatric team, one social worker is needed for every 2,500 children. This proportion would be adequate in cities where population is condensed. In rural areas where homes are scattered and time must be spent in travel, one worker to 1,000 unselected children is a generally accepted figure.

Considerable progress has been made in the development of this work throughout the country. If social service is important for the handling of problems of normal children, it is all the more important for those who are handicapped by intellectual retardation, and who, for that reason, require a greater measure of guidance. The social worker, understanding the point of view of the school, calls to her aid all available resources in studying the child's problems as seen in school and out, in tactfully bringing about improvements where needed in the family situation and home conditions, and in putting the child in touch with the right kind of neighborhood and community influences.

From the viewpoint of the backward pupil himself, the special class is a haven. It is in the regular grades that his intellectual and social limitations constantly stand out in such a way as to draw the jibes of fellow pupils and make him painfully conscious of his shortcomings. In the special class he finds himself among his peers; he can keep up with his group; he may even excel. His individual aptitudes and interests are considered and he is given an opportunity for self-expression in a type of work in which he takes a natural interest. All this leads to satisfaction and is reflected in decreased truancy and general improvement in behavior. Another factor that leads to better social adjustment is that the child is not subjected to the frustrations he suffers outside of the classroom when he is among his equals. It is believed that endless disappointments and rebuffs in neighborhood contacts are largely accountable for the unsocial behavior observed in many retarded children.

Because of the nature of the work, and the greater necessity for attention to individual pupils, it is recognized that the size of special classes must be appreciably smaller than that of regular grades. The general practice has been to limit the enrollment in special classes to from 15 to 18 pupils.

Most cities have established one or more special classes in a number of public schools. A few others have organized special schools to which all retarded children in the system go. Both methods have advantages and disadvantages. The former method has, for example, the advantages of accessibility and of some degree of contact with normal children. The latter permits better grouping of children and better equipment. A combination of the two methods is sometimes found, as where an entire floor of one public school is used for retarded children. A common practice in large cities is to provide special classes for young children in a number of public schools, so that small children can attend schools in their immediate neighborhoods. Older children, of Junior High School age, are accommodated in more centralized classes.

Any method of organization must first take practical matters such as distance and transportation into consideration. All methods try to avoid stigmatizing the child. Each has its own ardent proponents, though, in general, the trend is away from segregation in special schools. If organization and conduct of the classes are rightly managed, little or no stigma attaches to children attending them.

The Differentiated Curriculum

Special class instruction differs in kind, as well as in degree, from that of the graded class. The most conspicuous differentiating factor is the emphasis special classes place upon functional training. The curriculum is not watered down but differentiated in a way to catch the interest of the child. In general, retarded children can work more successfully with objects and materials than with words and numbers. Miss Elise Martens, in writing of curriculum adjustments for the retarded,[3] states that the aim of education is the same as for the normal—namely, to teach them how to live better. Of factors in social efficiency the most important are self-expression and self-control, the first of which must not be allowed to interfere with the second.

Education is directed to achievement in knowledge, occupational life, social relations, and use of leisure time. The child must have experience day by day in situations that give him the knowledge and disposition to keep well, and that give him the social ease and ability to make and keep friends and to live as a contributing member of family and community. He must be taught, if possible, to earn the necessities of life and to manage wisely the money he earns.

Miss Martens outlines curriculum suggestions for children of various levels of ability. For children with a mental age of below six, the "three R's" are omitted. Habit training is stressed, such as personal cleanliness, toileting, eating, and health measures.. Social experience is encouraged by discussions about parents, siblings, classmates, safety, the policeman. Sense training includes

[3] Martens, *Curriculum Adjustments for the Mentally Retarded.*

recognizing one's name, matching colors and shapes, completing picture puzzles, studying natural phenomena such as sky and trees, identifying objects by sound, smell, or touch, and recognizing food by taste. Speech training is directed to functional communication. Muscular coordination is cultivated through rhythm exercises, marching and dancing to music, games and practice on equipment, such as on rungs of a ladder. Nature study concerns common pets, flowers, trees, weather, and seasons. Manual training begins with hammering nails into blocks of wood, carrying household articles, stringing beads, cutting paper and cloth.

All of the projects are used as a foundation for oral language. They are found to be more effective if planned around a center of interest.

For children with mental age above six, reading, writing, and number work are introduced, as are units of experience in the arts, civics, health, physical training. Manual activities such as shop, kitchen or laundry work prepare for homemaking. Such units of experience are not taught at random, but are based on the common needs of living, and are graded according to the spontaneous interests of the children, the level of manual dexterity, and mental comprehension.

For beginners the modern trend is not to teach specific skills but to give a background in the use of equipment of many kinds. Obviously specialized training for all the manifold types of unskilled or skilled employment cannot be provided, but training can be related to basic operations, with special attention to those which appear to afford the most likely employment opportunities. The ability to work with fellow pupils may be developed in a project that requires the participation of several students.

It is recognized that if habits of disappointment and failure are allowed to persist they may become deeply fixed in the personality. There must be sufficient repetition of experience to form the attitudes desired. Abstract generalization must give way to concrete applications. "Mere suggestions will not do the work."

For older retarded children, physical development and social maturity are the major considerations in planning work. The curriculum of a junior or senior high school, or of a four-year high school, can be adapted for one or two pupils or for a whole class.

Since the majority of special class pupils will earn a living with their hands, manual training must develop good work habits and skills that will later help in securing jobs. If proper equipment is lacking the teacher uses what is at hand. Manual work is regarded as one of the most satisfying experiences, as well as a valuable preparation for occupation. The selection of the type of manual work is determined by mental and chronological age, resources and equipment.

Parent Education

A valuable extension of special class education is the movement to help parents of retarded children understand and deal constructively with the problems of home training. Groups for parent training have been organized not only by public schools but by a few institutions and on a larger scale by local units of the National Association for Retarded Children.

The first parent education series conducted by the Bureau for Children with Retarded Mental Development, New York City, demonstrated the value of such a service. The program was centered on home training of young children as a prerequisite for school entrance and school success. Topics included: the development of proper eating and toilet habits, and of the ability to put on and take off outer clothing and to walk up and down stairs; the emotional needs of the retarded child; discipline; the directing of interest toward toys and games; and the place of the retarded child in the home.

Early in the series stress was laid on underlying considerations: that likenesses of children are more important than deviations; that family life must not be distorted by the slow-learning child; that good personality is basic to successful living; that parents must learn to sublimate their feeling of inadequacy, and attempt to give the retarded child the same security and wholesome training as would be given to any other child. It was clearly brought out that academic achievement is not the criterion for a good life adjustment.

Literature helpful to parents was provided and studies were assigned, such as methods of building habits or controlling temper tantrums. Parents were asked to write down their most pressing problems which the leaders checked for frequency, and used for later discussions. After eight weekly sessions it was evident that parents had gained greatly in confidence and skill.

In Flint, Michigan, the staff of the Lapeer State Home and Training School, the Child Guidance Clinic, and a representative of the school system compiled a list of parents of retarded children under ten who had been excluded from school and those on waiting lists of institutions for the retarded. Parents were invited to a meeting. A planning committee outlined a course of study based on the expressed interests of the parents. This was worked into a complete prospectus. Several sessions each were devoted to such areas as causes and effects of retardation, emotional needs of the child, relationships of the retarded child in family and neighborhood, what parents can do to meet the child's needs, what the community can do for the retarded child. Books, charts, films, and field trips supplemented the class discussions.

Trends noted at the end of the first semester were relief from feelings of guilt, reduction of hostility toward the public schools, disappearance of fear of the state training school, better acceptance of their retarded children, interest in developing a cooperative nursery school, formation of a chapter of the Michigan Association of Parents of Mentally Retarded Children.

Other results of great value soon followed. The Board of Education of the Flint Public Schools authorized setting up two rooms for the severely retarded, and has worked out a flexible relationship with the State Home, facilitating the best placement of the child for training.

A group of parents formed a car pool so that five children

could attend the day school program at the Lapeer State Home, twenty miles away. Work was begun with the City Recreation Department to plan a summer recreation program for retarded children.

The second semester of the course centered around clinical discussions of the children of parents enrolled. It was conducted by a clinic team and was clearly successful.

Service in Rural Areas

Generally speaking, the best results in the organization of special classes in country areas have been secured through promotion and supervision by state agencies such as state departments of education and of mental hygiene. The state-wide clinic system developed in 1921 in Massachusetts to aid the special class program furnished an effective model.

When it became evident that a large number of the children examined by the Traveling School Clinics were referred not because of retardation but because of a behavior or social problems, the Out Patient and Child Guidance Clinics expanded their programs. They are now used for consultation and treatment, as well as diagnostic purposes. This system has the great advantage of providing psychiatric, psychological, and social service for schools that have no personnel for study and selection of children who need special class opportunities.

A similar method was developed in New York at about the same time and other states also have followed this pattern. California gets the same result by a different method. County service funds enable county superintendents to employ expert assistants for the smaller schools in their districts. Indiana introduced another system, now used in a number of states. Cooperative boards furnish special service for eight or ten consolidated school districts.

Dr. Arnold Gesell, Director of the Gesell Institute at New Haven, rendered a most useful service years ago in the publication of a handbook for teachers, showing how the problem of training the deficient child can be met in rural sections where special class facilities are not available. Dr. Gesell asserted: "There is no excuse for neglecting a mentally deficient child, whether he is in a crowded classroom of a large city, or in some village or country school." [4] The individual method outlined is briefly that of arranging special activities for retarded children which can be carried on within the regular classroom under the supervision of the regular teacher, but apart from the regular class work. The consolidation of rural schools favors organization of more special classes in country areas.

Results

How do these retarded children who have received special training in the public schools turn out? It is not until this question has been answered that the success of the public school as a leading agency in the mental deficiency program can be fully judged. Many studies have been made in an attempt to answer this question.

Among early inquiries was a follow-up study of the graduates of special classes in New York City made in 1925. The group studied consisted of 400 former special class pupils, 218 boys and 182 girls, who had been out of school from one to four years. All but ten of the children were found to be living at home, or in their own establishments if married. Home conditions in 36½ percent of the cases were good, in 42½ percent fair, in 19 percent poor, in 2 percent unknown.

A total of 259 (162 boys and 97 girls), or 64 percent, were employed for wages. Others, unemployed at the time of the study, had proved their ability to hold positions, so that in all, 334, or 83 percent, of the 400 boys and girls were regarded as employable. Four, or 1 percent, had been committed to institutions; and one boy in prison at the time of the study was later released and went home to live.

[4] Gesell, *The Retarded Child: How to Help Him.*

The U.S. Children's Bureau long ago made a study of the work histories of some 1,000 young men and women who had formerly been enrolled in the special classes for mental defectives in the cities of Detroit, Rochester, Newark, Cincinnati, Oakland, San Francisco, and Los Angeles.[5] Over half of all the jobs held by both boys and girls were in manufacturing and mechanical industries. The larger proportion were employed as semiskilled operatives in factories. The employers when interviewed, rated 78 percent of the boys and 80 percent of the girls as satisfactory in the performance of their work. The unsatisfactory work was largely in apprenticeships in skilled trades, clerical occupations, and messenger services.

As to conduct, it was found that 14 percent of the group had court records. The work records of this delinquent group showed that they had much less employment than those who had not fallen into delinquency. The conclusions reached by the Children's Bureau were as follows: "The study as a whole would seem to indicate that there is a place for subnormal boys and girls in industry. . . . The percentages of promotions for the different intelligence groups and wage increases from first to later job, show that ability to progress increased with a higher intelligence quotient. The fact that so many young persons of less than average mentality were able to earn a livelihood is doubtless due in part to the training given them while in the special classes, in good habit formation, and in a right attitude toward work."

Later surveys show corresponding results. In a paper called "Follow-Up of 1,000 Non-Academic Boys," [6] Dr. W. J. McIntosh describes the histories of boys from the Jarvis School for Boys, Toronto. This is a trade school for nonacademic boys, admitted after intelligence tests have been made by the Mental Health Division of the Department of Public Health.

The survey included a ten-year period from January, 1936 to December, 1946. Cases were unselected except that the first 1,000 located who had spent six months or more at the school were

---

[5] Fourteenth Annual Report of Children's Bureau, pp. 12–14.
[6] See *Journal of Exceptional Children* (March, 1949).

chosen. Ages were from sixteen to thirty years, but 66.8 percent were under twenty-four years, and 54.7 percent were twenty-one years old or under. The I.Q. range was from 46 to over 100. Using sixteen as the normal adult mental age, 65.2 percent had I.Q.s between 66 and 80, that is, had mental ages of eleven and twelve years.

Only 2.2 percent were unemployed; 1.1 percent were in penal institutions; 44.2 percent had been in the armed forces; 37.8 percent were earning as much as the average industrial worker in Toronto at the time. Men with I.Q.s under 60 showed a higher percentage of unemployment than the group as a whole, but many were steady and self-supporting.

A comparison of wages was made by groups with differing I.Q.s. It was found that a difference of 10 points in the I.Q. made little difference in the amount of money earned. Other factors such as emotional stability and personal drive were as important as even 20 points in I.Q. within the range of 65–95. It is pointed out that these personality qualities are more amenable to educational procedures than is the I.Q.

In the group there were 52 men with I.Q.s under 60 and adult mental age of seven to nine years. Only three were married. Unemployment was 13.5 percent as compared with 2.2 percent for the whole group of 1,000. However, of the 52 more handicapped men, 75.8 percent were self-supporting, an achievement which appears to justify the specialized education they received.

While the Jarvis boys were not found in professions or in complex business positions, they entered a great variety of useful occupations and retained their positions as well as the average worker.

A few more studies can properly be discussed here. A group of 121 men and women who had left special classes in the Detroit public schools in 1941 was studied in 1953.[7] Of 95 men, 27 percent were in unskilled jobs, 34 percent were in semiskilled jobs;

[7] "Economic Adjustment of 121 Adults Formerly Students in Classes for Mental Retardates," by Allen Bobroff, M.Ed. in *American Journal of Mental Deficiency* (January, 1956).

16 percent were in skilled jobs; 15 percent were in military service or miscellaneous jobs; 8 percent were unemployed.

Of 29 women, 14 percent were in unskilled jobs, 14 percent were in semiskilled jobs, 14 percent were in skilled jobs; 58 percent were doing housework.

The men earned mean wages of some $2.09 an hour when the city-wide average of production workers was $2.23 an hour. Seventy-five percent had held their positions for over three years, some for as long as twelve years. Only four of the entire group (3 percent) had received welfare aid.

A long-term study was made by Charles in 1953.[8] This was a follow-up of 206 special class pupils in Lincoln, Nebraska, adjudged mentally deficient in 1935. The average age of the group was forty-two years, and for the 151 located the record was excellent. Eighty-three percent had been self-supporting part of the time, and most were regularly employed.

Severely retarded children also show the favorable results of schooling. A study of a sampling of 2,640 former pupils in classes for the trainable in New York City public schools from 1929 to 1956 was reported in 1958 by Dr. Gerhart Saenger, "Adjustment of Severely Retarded Adults in the Community," New York State Interdepartmental Health Resources Board, 1958. The age range was from seventeen to forty years. It was found that 1,742 (about two-thirds) of the group were living in the community; 686 (about one-fourth) were in institutions; 212 had died since leaving school. Of those living at home, most appeared to have made a good adjustment to family living and 27 worked for pay at simple jobs.

These studies of the after-school careers of the mentally deficient definitely indicate that the large majority of special class graduates are able to take their places in community life as decent working citizens who are in no sense social burdens. Many of these graduates may be regarded as social and industrial assets. These results of special class work emphasize the great impor-

[8] Don C. Charles, "Ability and Accomplishment of Persons Earlier Judged Mentally Deficient." *Genetic Psychology Monographs,* 1953.

tance of making such training facilities available to all retarded children in our school systems.

When the public schools have provided an adequate number of effective special classes, supplemented by competent psychological, psychiatric, and social service, then a large part of the "problem of mental deficiency" will have been solved.

XVII. Vocational Training and Employment

THE mid-twentieth century saw the beginning of modern programs on a large scale for vocational guidance, training, and skilled placement of the mentally retarded.

The excellent work of institution social workers in finding jobs for former patients has always been carried on against great odds. Furthermore, since only a small percentage of the retarded ever get to institutions, their programs have necessarily been limited in scope.

The public schools also face limits in vocational training and placement. With few exceptions schools lack space and equipment for trade training. Even schools with the best facilities cannot reproduce the circumstances of paid employment. In place of the friendly teacher, there is the "boss" who wants results. Instead of one or more hours at a job, there are eight hours. In school the program is varied but in industry there may be monotony. Just as serious are differences in social settings. In school the retarded pupil is surrounded by others of his kind, all well known to him. In industry he is with strangers, not all of them too kind. A remark or action that in school would bring only a reprimand may mean in industry the loss of a job. One girl, being helped by a counselor after repeated failures, exclaimed, "No one ever told me not to argue."

Of the current trends in preparing retarded young people for a useful place in the world, three seem of special promise: more attention to personality; more realistic training in public schools and institutions; greater cooperation between schools, institutions, and training and placing agencies. The time has long passed when the standard recommendation was "routine work under supervision." The retarded often stand routine better than the normal, but personality, interests, motor control, adaptive capacity, and fatigue tolerance are now given major consideration. Special classes have dropped "busy work" and the final goal of handiwork is some degree of skill leading to possible employment or useful occupation.

Increasing cooperation between agencies can be found in many places. In New York which has special units in junior high schools, vocational training curricula have been devised based on data assembled by teachers who conducted surveys. Some of the results are as follows: (1) information has been collected on low-level jobs; (2) a job analysis schedule has been compiled and published; (3) information on unskilled and semiskilled jobs in the food and garment trades has been compiled and published.[1]

The Vocational Adjustment Bureau

A noteworthy demonstration of the needs and possibilities of industrial placement was made by the Vocational Adjustment Bureau of New York City, established in 1919 and directed by Dr. Emily T. Burr. It was the purpose of this Bureau to place in suitable employment women and girls from fourteen to thirty years of age, handicapped by reason of mental deficiency, personality problems, or delinquency. About half the girls assisted were retarded, and an additional fourth were graded as dull normals.

The Bureau went about its task scientifically by thorough study, both of the individual and of the job. Each girl was given a general intelligence test, a mechanical assembly test, various trade tests, and other special aptitude tests, in order to determine for what type and grade of work she was best fitted. The Bureau did much preliminary work in endeavoring to fit the girl for employment. For example, it was found that many of the girls

[1] *Occupational Education* (October, November, December, 1949).

needed to be taught how to use scissors, to do plain sewing, and other such fundamentals before being referred to positions. Accuracy, motor coordination, and punctuality were specially stressed. If physical ailments or personality difficulties were present, the assistance of medical and psychiatric clinics was secured. Social service visits were also made to the homes in many cases in an endeavor to adjust situations there that interfered with progress.

The Bureau established in November, 1925, a therapeutic experimental workroom for the rehabilitation of those who, because of nervousness and emotional instability, were incapacitated for regular employment. As soon as these girls were sufficiently recovered, they were placed by the Bureau in jobs suited to their limited strength and ability. A second workroom was later opened to which girls often progressed from the therapeutic workroom. Both the small and the large workshop were put on a paying basis in the manufacture of decorative wastebaskets, shoe-trees, and other articles which were sold through department stores. Considering the limitations of the workers, this was a remarkable achievement.

The Bureau also inaugurated the policy, within the limitations of its funds, of awarding scholarships in small sums to promising girls whereby they could meet the tuition expenses of special short training courses. One girl, for example, was enabled to spend two weeks in learning to operate an adding machine, another was sent to a beauty-parlor school.

The Bureau did a great deal of excellent work in the study of employment opportunities for handicapped girls. Staff members with a knowledge of industrial processes went into the plants of many different industries to determine the degree of attention, dexterity, uniformity, speed, judgment, perseverance, color perception, and tactual discrimination required in different operations. Among the types of industries studied were power-machine operating, candy-making and packing, underwear manufacturing, and many others. Many industrial establishments co-operated in making these studies; others were carried on with the cooperation of the New York City Continuation Schools. Manufacturers often furnished free material for training purposes. At times they accepted girls from the Bureau knowing it would cut down the training, for which supervisors often had little patience. In effect, this arrangement transferred the training period to the workshop.

A number of factory employees were given trade tests so that it might be revealed, by a study of the workers actually on the job, what degree of mental alertness and other traits were demanded in different positions. It was found that the minimum mental age at which a girl is capable of industrial adjustment is six years. Girls of this limited capacity, provided they were sufficiently stable emotionally, were successfully employed in packing powder puffs and other simple articles not easily damaged, polishing mirrors for women's pocketbooks, and trimming leather goods. Girls with a mental age from seven to eight years gained employment in assembling electrical parts, carding buttons, dressing dolls, pasting, and as errand girls or institutional domestics. Girls of the eight- to nine-year mental level did well in addressing envelopes, beading dresses, checking hats, clipping threads, working on flowers and feathers, performing domestic service, and operating elevators. Girls from nine to ten years mental age, but none under that level, succeeded in assembling radio parts, cleaning dresses, making artificial flowers, manicuring, selling in five-and-ten-cent stores, and wrapping parcels.[2] Girls with a mental age over ten largely found employment at the same tasks listed for those with a mental level of from nine to ten years, but they, on the whole, remained longer in the same employment, and were less likely to be laid off in a slack season. These classifications all assumed that emotional factors did not unduly affect the girl's personality.[3]

This analysis of minimum age levels was a valuable guide in making successful placements, and in assuring as far as possible

[2] Emily Burr, "Adjustment of the Feebleminded in Industry," in *Journal of Psycho-Asthenics*, 31:42–53.

[3] Emily Burr, "Minimum Levels of Accomplishment" (1931). (Out of print.)

that a girl would not be placed in a type of work beyond her mental ability and skill. Among other important research undertaken by the Bureau was the preparation of a calendar [4] which set forth graphically the busy and slack periods throughout the year in each industry. This calendar was of great assistance in planning for the year-round employment of girls who entered seasonal trades.

Many later studies show how the results of research guide vocational agencies in avoiding the hardship and waste incurred by training and placing retarded young people in unsuitable jobs. The Vocational Adjustment Bureau furnished a remarkable example of what can be accomplished by training mentally retarded persons to a level where they could hold their own in the labor market. It closed in 1946 at the time the Office of Vocational Rehabilitation was developing its program.

Workshops

Training workshops for the retarded are urgently needed everywhere, but have been very slow to develop. What few we have offer services for the most part excellent in quality but almost negligible in quantity. Most of them were opened to the retarded after 1950. They operate four or five hours a day and in general are not self-supporting. Their purpose is not only to give occupational training but also to aid in personality adjustment.

Local units of the National Association for Retarded Children are actively promoting development of workshops, and are operating training centers in a number of cities. Examples are the centers conducted by the Association for the Help of Retarded Children, the New York state branch of the national association. When the first center was opened in 1953, it was the only sheltered shop for the retarded in New York City, with its population of some 8,000,000. By 1957 organizations affiliated

[4] Emily Burr and Catherine Treat, "Industrial Calendar" (1936).

with the National Association had sponsored sixty-seven workshops throughout the country, and twice this number were in the planning stage.

The Goodwill Industries, established in over a hundred cities, though organized to aid the physically handicapped, accept the mentally deficient to a limited extent. In Cincinnati it opened an occupational training center for the retarded in the spring of 1952, and a Work Adjustment Shop in 1953. The retarded have their own supervisor and place of work, but have the benefit of the counseling service, business experience, and contract procurement of the larger agency. This plan of organizing a shop for the retarded in an existing center for the handicapped may indicate a future trend.

The Rehabilitation Center for the Disabled in New York City may be cited as an example of an excellent service limited by its budget to small numbers. Established in 1924 for the physically handicapped, it has through its liberal policy included a proportion of mentally handicapped clients. Four workshops under experienced supervisors, and facilities for office work, offer training in a number of occupations. Psychiatric consultation and social casework are available.

Two interesting pilot projects of this Center have been conducted jointly with the Division of Vocational Rehabilitation, and showed a need to sample other job areas for the mentally retarded. Examination of unskilled occupations in institutions indicated a large number of jobs suitable. Clients were selected by the Division, and training was conducted by the Center. Courses of six or eight weeks were given in such occupations as nurse's aid, ward maid, kitchen helper, or porter. A more advanced course trained for making beds, cleaning rooms, and washing patient's face and hands. Room, equipment, and routine used in training were exactly like those in a hospital. Of 14 in the course all but one secured jobs in an institution or small hospital.

The second pilot study grew out of a survey of the button industry. A four-week trial period determined the client's ability to handle the machine and material. Thereafter the client progressed with emphasis on production. All who completed the course obtained employment.

A different type of intermediate training, equivalent to a sheltered workshop, is provided by a few state schools for the retarded. In some cases there is an arrangement by which boys and girls work in neighborhood industries for periods of six weeks or more. They may be tried for short periods at a number of different jobs. In this way aptitudes and interests are found and work tolerance evaluated before a permanent placement is attempted.

A similar type of sheltered training, in which piece work of various kinds is sent to the institutions by local industries, has also been found practical. In such cases the heads of different shops at the state school supervise the work in cooperation with personnel of the industry. When training is completed, the patient may be ready for parole and a place in competitive employment.

Office of Vocational Rehabilitation

The Office of Vocational Rehabilitation of the Federal Security Agency, offers vocational training and placement for mental defectives through its local branches. Public Law 113, enacted in 1943, extended a service previously of limited nature, to all classes of vocationally handicapped persons. The program is conducted by state education departments which have passed enabling laws to qualify for funds, and is administered entirely by state agencies in each of the forty-eight states, the District of Columbia, Puerto Rico, Hawaii and Alaska.

Amendments passed in 1954 have greatly strengthened the law. In the words of one writer it is "now possible for states to offer better services to more people." Among new advantages are: (1) the provision for expansion of rehabilitation facilities; (2) the authorization for programs to train personnel, of which there is a serious shortage; (3) grants for aid to nonprofit agencies for rehabilitation services; and (4) grants to state, public, or nonprofit agencies for research and special projects or facilities that might lead to solving problems of rehabilitating the handicapped.

The OVR helps handicapped persons, including the retarded, who may need a variety of services before they are ready for employment.

Nine basic services are offered: (1) medical, psychological, and, if indicated, psychiatric evaluation; (2) individual counsel and guidance; (3) medical, surgical, psychiatric, and hospital care if needed to remove or reduce disability; (4) artificial appliances, such as hearing aids, eyeglasses, braces; (5) preadjustment, pre-vocational, and vocational training, in schools, on the job, or otherwise; (6) maintenance and transportation if necessary during treatment or training; (7) occupational tools, equipment, and licenses as necessary; (8) selective placement, within physical and mental limitations; and (9) follow-up after placement.

Three studies are cited to illustrate various ways of working out a rehabilitation program for the retarded in the community.

NEW YORK CITY   The New York City District Office of the Division of Vocational Rehabilitation [5] received its first application for rehabilitation of a mental defective in 1946. The agency provides diagnostic service, vocational counseling and training, job placement, and job follow-up. In general all persons over fourteen years of age are eligible for service if they have a mental or physical handicap. In practice, however, the program is focused on "service-feasible" clients, namely, those whose needs will be met by vocational rehabilitation. Feasibility is determined by a complete mental, physical, social, and emotional evaluation of each applicant. "Service-unfeasible" clients are referred, as far as possible, to other community agencies.

A study was made of 400 mental defectives who applied for service between July 1, 1947 and July 1, 1949, all of whom could be studied from acceptance to closure. The study included only

[5] Condensed from *Vocational Rehabilitation of the Mentally Retarded* (Federal Security Agency, 1950) with permission of author, Leonard W. Rockower.

persons over fifteen not in schools or institutions. Of the number, 142 were finally classified as rehabilitated, and 258 as unfeasible. There were 319 boys in the group and 81 girls. The great majority were from fifteen to twenty-four years old. Intelligence quotients ranged from below 50 to over 75, the mode of the rehabilitated group being 62, and the mode of the unfeasible group, 52. Almost 50 percent of the whole number showed physical or mental disabilities in addition to retardation. These ranged from minor conditions to serious disorders. Of the 400 studied, 264 had never worked before and 136 had had some work experience.

About half of the referrals came from the U.S. Employment Service and from public and private schools. A little more than one-fourth came from family and group work agencies or hospitals and health agencies.

In a cooperative project between the Bureau for Children with Retarded Mental Development of the public school system, and the Rehabilitation Agency, information was shared. The school summarized important facts and conclusions which greatly assisted the Agency in developing work plans.

All applicants had the benefit of vocational counseling the purpose of which was to evolve a vocational plan which would include all services leading to job placement. It was found that mentally retarded persons require occupation preparation in specific areas. (Though only 65 percent of the rehabilitated group requested vocational training, 80 percent were considered to be in need of it.) A canvass of the city showed that while many agencies offer vocational training in the skilled trades, very few prepare the mentally retarded for placement in unskilled work.

The 142 clients classed as rehabilitated were employed chiefly in unskilled or semiskilled occupations of great variety: machine operator, shipping clerk, messenger, elevator operator, porter, laborer, paint sprayer, cleaner, presser, packer, sorter, kitchen helper, etc. About half the jobs were obtained by the rehabilitation counselor or an employment service and about 40 percent by parents and other relatives.

A follow-up study made in 1950 showed that of 142 rehabilitated, 85 were still in the job where originally placed, six were in other jobs, and 30 were unemployed. One had been institutionalized and on 20 no data could be found. Of the unfeasible group about two-thirds were unemployed. In both groups those employed had averaged considerably longer on the job than they had in other jobs before applying for rehabilitation service.

The study is well worth discussing in more detail, but since New York City can hardly be considered typical of other localities, the conclusions reached may be of more interest. Some of these briefly summarized are: (1) The number and variety of agencies referring mental defectives suggests the widespread character of the problem; (2) Some 25 percent were deemed not immediately placeable, though they had come from schools where they had had specialized training; (3) Though secondary disabilities were present in nearly 50 percent of the study group, referring agencies showed little understanding of their implications for employment; (4) Inadequacies of home environment had produced socially immature persons hardly able to assume responsibility; (5) The study group sought almost immediate job placement, but evaluation of needs did not always coincide with the kind of service requested; (6) Community services for the mentally deficient in New York City were so inadequate that while 74 percent of the study group required sheltered workshop service only 1 percent could be so placed; (7) Due to lack of resources many "unfeasible" clients are unable to contribute, though many could, if given the needed assistance; (8) Employment stability correlates directly with vocational counseling and supervision and contributes to personal and social improvements as well as to vocational adjustment; (9) Parents are frequently a major problem in planning and need skilled guidance in more realistic acceptance of their children's disabilities; (10) There is need to inform professional groups and the public about the occupational assets of the retarded, and to make industry aware of an important but untapped worker resource.

MICHIGAN   A report from the Michigan Office of Vocational Rehabilitation [6] notes that in a five-year period beginning in 1944 this agency rehabilitated 433 persons whose primary disability was mental retardation.

An early experiment of the agency was undertaken by the Jackson office at the suggestion of the Coldwater Home & Training School where overcrowding made it desirable to consider rehabilitation of a selected group. The cases were referred as a group and were served so far as possible through group training and supervision.

The group consisted of 12 men and 10 women between eighteen and twenty-four years of age, who had been institutionalized for some years. The I.Q.s ranged from 50 to 70 for all but 2 who, though with higher I.Q., had personality problems. All had had the advantages of training and treatment at the Home.

Through canvassing and advertising, enough homes were found for a good selection, and the project was explained to prospective landladies. The counselor then made calls on industrial and business establishments to insure suitable training and placement. Instructions were given to clients who understood that abuse of privileges might mean their return to the institution. Several days were spent with the group to give them orientation, and tours were planned to acquaint them with the city.

Personal interviews were arranged with employers. Some clients were placed in industry where they were taught to operate machines or do assembly work. Several were placed in bakeries and laundries. The counselor made regular visits to employers and in 1947 reported: "The fact that after one and a half years, out of a group of 22 clients, there was only 1 failure, indicates that rehabilitation on a selective basis of institutional cases appears justified."

In 1950 a follow-up study was made. The counselor reported that 13 of 22 clients were satisfactorily employed and making

[6] Condensed from *Vocational Rehabilitation of the Mentally Retarded* (Federal Security Agency, 1950) with permission of the author, Miss Jane Potts.

good adjustments. Three were making their own way, but were not steady workers. Three were classed as failures, and three had left the community.

Throughout the experiment the Office of Vocational Rehabilitation worked with authorities of the institution from which the clients came, furnishing a splendid example of cooperative planning. Another notable feature was that the clients, carefully selected, made excellent adjustments in the community direct from the institution. In this case a community agency carried on the home finding, job hunting, training, and supervision that in most cases is done by the institution during the parole period.

In Detroit and in Wayne County a cooperative plan has been worked out with the Division of Special Education of the Detroit Public Schools. It has therefore been possible to carry on a more concentrated program in Detroit and in Wayne County than in other parts of the state.

At the age of fifteen years or more, boys and girls from the Special Trade School are selected for referral to the Office of Vocational Rehabilitation. On clients referred by public schools and institutions, psychological evaluations are furnished as part of the referral. In other cases tests are made either by the staff or by psychologists of other agencies. Such service may be on a fee basis, or may be contributed by the employing agency.

The I.Q. is not the only basis for determining eligibility or feasibility but it has been found that the services of persons with I.Q.s below 40 are not marketable in the community, though they may be useful at home or in an institution. In the case of I.Q.s from 40 to 55, possibilities are relative, some can be rehabilitated and some cannot. Other factors such as personality and socialization may make the difference. Clients with I.Q.s from 55 to 75 are in general feasible for rehabilitation service, and 60 percent to 75 percent of referrals are in this zone. In the range of I.Q.s from 75 to 85 or over, few are eligible for the specialized service, since their disability does not constitute a vocational handicap.

On-the-job training has been found to be the best means of

entering clients in employment. This method is seldom possible in large factories or on a contract basis where a fee is paid for training. In smaller shops a fee may be paid to compensate the employer for teaching the applicants. Such a training period may be from two weeks to two months or more. During this time maintenance and transportation costs may be paid by the agency.

Sometimes an employment opportunity may be developed by the group method. In an unusual project, a group of young women were successfully trained as a team to clean and maintain an apartment house. One acted as supervisor, each of the others had her speciality, such as cleaning kitchens, bathrooms, or rugs.

The tentative conclusions of the Michigan Office of Vocational Rehabilitation are in part as follows: (1) On-the-job training has been found to be the most suitable method for training the mentally retarded; (2) The counselor had to devote more time per case to the average mentally retarded than to the average of other handicapped groups; (3) The transition from school to initial employment represents a critical period in rehabilitation; (4) The effectiveness of the program seems highly dependent on the cooperation of community and interested agencies; (5) Selected institutional cases seem to make more satisfactory adjustments than referrals from schools, or employment and other agencies perhaps because they are older, have had more training and have been more carefully selected; (6) Above a certain mental level, personal adjustment is a greater determinant than I.Q. in predicting success and many adjustment failures seem to be the result of poor home background; (7) Socialization is an important factor in employability; (8) The mentally retarded seem to adjust in repetitive jobs, which those of average ability find monotonous.

MINNESOTA In Minnesota the state division of Vocational Rehabilitation [7] functions through one branch office and five

---

[7] Condensed from *Vocational Rehabilitation of the Mentally Retarded* (Federal Security Agency, 1950) with permission of authors, Miss Florence I. Haasarud and Miss Sara W. Moore.

district offices. The branch in Minneapolis is maintained in cooperation with the Minneapolis Board of Education. The program with the mentally retarded described below began late in 1946. Though the Division extends service to the mentally retarded in other parts of the state, the Minneapolis office was the first to work out an arrangement with the public schools.

Special classes were provided for the mentally retarded through the ninth grade. Supervision in personality and group adjustment was offered as well as school subjects. The majority of students leave school at sixteen years, with little practical training for earning a living. Since employers prefer workers over eighteen years old, many who left school at sixteen years were unemployed till they were eighteen. It was felt important for the school to bridge the gap between sixteen and eighteen by devoting time to academic and vocational training adapted to individual needs, thus greatly increasing chances of employment.

While evaluation and interviewing proceeded, authorities conferred on additional facilities for training. A special class called "Related Subjects" was established at Vocational High School. The class provided each individual with the academic training required in his shop work. For instance, a boy training in upholstering would need to know how to figure measurements, and to read and write the names of materials. A girl in power sewing would need less mathematics but should be able to read and write at least well enough to fill out application blanks. In addition to academic training the teacher coaches students in personal matters. The program was so successful that another Related Subjects class was organized in the following year.

In general rehabilitation counselors must depend on other agencies for training, since the Vocational Rehabilitation Divisions do not attempt to set up their own training services. The counselor must accept prevailing conditions and also make suggestions for changes. The Minneapolis office is in a favorable position because its supervisor is also consultant for special education in the public schools.

A first assumption is that most of those in the public schools are potentially employable, but need help in training and placement. A second assumption is that few generalizations about job placement can be made for the whole group. Aptitudes and interests cover a wide range. Another assumption is that personal traits are highly important in determining success.

Students in special classes range in I.Q. between 50 and 80. Aptitude testing was organized in 1946 as a joint project of the Special Education Division and the State Rehabilitation Division. The vocational rehabilitation counselor secured the names of mentally retarded students approaching sixteen years. A Board of Education psychologist assisted in testing and evaluating prospective clients. Since standard tests were not well adapted for the purpose, their results were not considered the most important factor in deciding what to recommend. Cumulative school records and personal reports from the school were considered valuable. In every case parents were consulted as to plans. Recommendations were made in view of facilities available, as well as the training desirable, if available.

Based on comprehensive studies there was a division of mentally retarded students at the junior high school level into three groups: 1) those to be trained in junior high school; 2) those to be placed in employment; 3) those to be trained in senior high school.

Length of training varies from a few weeks to three years, as needed. When the student appears to be ready for employment, an effort is made to find him a job. Usually the student remains in school until a job is found. If he makes a satisfactory job adjustment over a period of time, his case will be closed as rehabilitated. Some clients do not fit into a particular job, and another must be found. Some will return to school for more training.

During a three year period ending July, 1949, 143 mentally retarded persons were rehabilitated into competitive employment. Conclusions based on this report include the following points: (1) When placed in suitable training, a great many older mentally retarded students become well adjusted and self-supporting; (2) They are not a homogenous group, and must be treated as individuals. The general areas where full development is needed are in personal qualities, academic subjects, and trade knowledge and skills. (3) There should be opportunity for mentally retarded persons to learn some of the specific skills of a trade, even though they are not capable of learning the entire trade. An I.Q. of 80 is used in Minneapolis as the dividing line between normal and retarded groups, but when compared as to personality, skill, and performance, the groups are found to divide quite differently. "A boy may be well trained in a trade and capable of holding a job, but if he is not capable of managing his personal life, he will not be a satisfactory employee or a good citizen."

Figures of the Federal Office of Vocational Rehabilitation show the tremendous effect that training has on earnings. A study of 592 retarded persons by Di Michael in 1951 showed that before rehabilitation they earned about $35,900 a year; after rehabilitation $922,400. In 1956 the OVR set new records. Of 756 retarded persons 96 percent were unemployed when accepted for rehabilitation. The group had earned about $32,100 annually. After rehabilitation their estimated annual earnings were $1,265,150.

The United States Employment Service

The United States Employment Service, under the Department of Labor, maintains offices in large cities, and county offices in rural areas. The Division for the Handicapped accepts the retarded for selective placement.

The program for study of the handicapped which led to the development of the Selective Placement plan was begun in 1936 in the St. Paul–Minneapolis center for the occupational analysis program of the U.S.E.S. Reduced to the simplest terms the service consists of the best matching of the applicant's abilities with the actual requirements of the job.

Policies are based on broad concepts. It is not assumed that all individuals with a specialized handicap are incapacitated to the same degree. It is assumed that the handicapped show individual characteristics of aptitudes and interests, and that jobs, even with the same title, vary widely from plant to plant.

On the administrative level, part-time or full-time technically trained personnel in each State give leadership to the program. Plans also provide for one or more trained persons in each local office to give selective placement service. All staff members are trained to recognize the need and to help promote the interests of the handicapped with employers.

The U.S.E.S. is specifically a job placement agency, rather than a training organization. The general practice is to give special service to the mentally retarded only during the period of adjustment to work.

An effort is made to secure records of applicants, such as those furnished by schools, with evaluations in respect to emotional and social maturity, manual dexterity, reading, and arithmetic. Also sought are reports on ability to follow directions, cooperation, and initiative.

When no reports are available, there may be difficulty in securing enough information to classify and place the applicant. Another difficulty encountered is the attitude of parents, which may be overprotective or utterly unrealistic. Some parents, for example, object to placement in an inferior job, such as messenger, or helper, even though it may be the only kind of work in which the client can succeed.

The public employment agency is dependent, like all employment agencies, on securing job openings from employers. The latter list jobs with the U.S.E.S. only because they expect a good selection of candidates. The same job may be listed with commercial agencies and the employer makes his selection from the referrals of all agencies. The employment service is thus in a competitive position in securing jobs. Referrals of handicapped persons must be of the same caliber as for those without handicap. Applicants must be qualified for the work in view, and must be able to compete in the working world. The need of an applicant for a job cannot be made the basis for referrals, because employers pay for skills, and are not primarily interested in needs.

Some Attendant Problems

INDEPENDENT JOB FINDING   It must not be assumed that any large number of mental defectives who hold jobs have been trained for them or placed by specialized agencies. The majority of those employed have found their own jobs, hit or miss. The U.S. Department of Labor made a study some years ago of 1,067 boys and girls formerly in special classes in seven cities. Of these 94 percent had been employed at some time after leaving school. Only 5 percent of the boys and 7 percent of the girls had had help from schools or employment agencies in securing their first jobs. Of the boys, 31 percent, and of the girls, 38 percent were assisted in job finding by relatives or friends. But more than half of the whole group had depended on their own efforts. That this situation, though improving, continues today is indicated by the reports of modern specialized agencies. The tremendous difference between blundering into a job and receiving skilled help in training and placement has been pointed out.

Considering their handicap, the ingenuity and persistence shown by the retarded in finding and keeping jobs is often remarkable. A few examples will illustrate this point. A boy of twenty, examined at a clinic, was found to have a mental age of three years and had never attended school. To the amazement of the staff, it was discovered that he had for several years been employed by a near-by hat factory, where he was well liked. His work consisted of preparing the lining of men's hats by dipping a brush in a stiffening mixture and then turning it around the band. This simple job he could do as fast as any normal person.

A girl formerly in a special class was found doing well in a small shop which manufactured dolls. Her task was to paint the dolls' eyes. A boy of eighteen who lived near the seashore went to nature for employment and dug worms for bait. Though seasonal, this venture made him nearly self-supporting.

Help from the family, when it can be secured, serves a double purpose. Too often one hears, "It is easier to do it myself." This, of course, means that parents are ignoring the training potentialities of simple home jobs and small errands that require a measure of responsibility. One of the greatest aids to the morale of parents is the feeling that they are helping the child. It is worthwhile for this reason alone to encourage parents to take an active part in training. A second reason is the great advantage to the retarded in sharing household duties from the early years.

An unusual success was scored by parents of a young man with a mental age of about nine years. During a shortage of postal clerks the parents trained him at home for several months on a single operation of sorting mail. The young man never learned to read connected passages but became very quick at picking out single words like Utica, Syracuse, Rochester so that he could put mail into the right sacks. He secured a job in the local Post Office and has kept it for twenty years. He will soon be eligible for a retirement pension. This case is so exceptional that it can hardly serve as an example of what can be accomplished by home training. It is cited only to show the possibilities for successes on a smaller scale.

The retarded, like many other young people, often take the first paid work that turns up. Without guidance, the jobs they pick up may be highly unsuitable. In a routine test of students in a school in a small town, it was found that an older boy who was driving the school bus had an I.Q. of 68. Although his handling of the bus and his management of the children were satisfactory, the school cancelled the arrangement because it was thought the school's insurance might be invalidated if it were known that a mentally retarded boy was employed. Of course the primary consideration was that if an emergency of any kind arose, the boy might not use good judgment and might endanger the children.

PROMOTIONS The subject of promotion deserves a special word. It is quite natural that a young person with limited mentality should expect promotions from time to time, just like

everybody else. The parents expect it, and often industrial programs are so adjusted that every employee has a chance to move
up on a fixed schedule.

It would be entirely wrong to assume that a mental defective
who does one job well can never be moved up. He may not be
working at his top capacity and possible promotions should be
considered. He cannot, however, be safely promoted on the
same basis as the average person. Experience with the retarded
has shown repeatedly that good work on one job is not a
guarantee, or even a promise of good work on a higher level.
Many disappointments and much ill feeling have resulted from
routine promotions.

A man forty-two years old was sent to a traveling clinic by
his employer, the manager of a laundry. This manager, recently
put in charge, was making a commendable effort to promote all
the old hands to better jobs. Personnel records showed that
Fred, the clinic patient, had been on the same job for fifteen years.
His work was to take clothing out of hot water and put it into
a rinsing vat. This he did contentedly with two paddles. Seeing
his long successful record, the manager immediately gave him
another job at higher wages. Fred could not do it, nor any of the
other assignments offered. He was miserably unhappy and begged
to be put back at his old job. The manager, full of good will,
but lacking in understanding, sent him to the clinic hoping that
"some little mental quirk" could be straightened out to Fred's
advantage. Examination showed a mental age of about five years,
with no special aptitudes. Not knowing how the manager would
react to such a report, the clinic merely recommended returning Fred to his former work, since he seemed well suited to it.

This case is a good illustration of another point—the value to
society of the mental defective with a stable personality. Fred
was living with his mother in a tiny house about two miles
outside the city where he worked. In the morning his mother
would give him a list of supplies needed. This he would leave
at a grocery store on his way to work. When he went home he
would pick up the groceries and pay for them out of his wages.

This arrangement had gone on for years. Fred entirely supported himself and his mother. They lived in a very humble way, but both were content and asked favors of no one.

In an earlier day it might have been thought best to place Fred in an institution because of his low I.Q. That would have meant the cost of institutional care for him, besides the use of a bed probably needed for an urgent case. It would also have meant the cost of relief for the mother, and loneliness for both.

Returning to the matter of unwise promotions, the case of Arnold, a high grade defective about twenty-three years old, may be described. Trained in a sheltered workshop, he secured a very simple clerical position with a large and progressive firm. He was doing well when a vacancy occurred in the photographic room. Arnold was promoted to fill it. The new job was easy, but not easy enough. Arnold became confused when he tried to put films into different baths. His supervisor labored with him but after several days gave up. Arnold was returned to his clerical job, which fortunately was still open. He was bitterly disappointed. He and his parents had told all their friends about his new position and good salary. The demotion was a severe blow. It might have had a worse result, as sometimes happens in such cases, but Arnold was not dismissed, and he did not throw up his job.

Developing Fields of Employment

Experience has shown that by far the largest number of retarded persons employed are placed in unskilled jobs. Vocational training is therefore directed toward unskilled and semiskilled work.

There is a definite trend toward service jobs. One survey indicates that in New York there are some 209,000 workers in the restaurant industry alone. Of these jobs probably half are within the ability of mentally handicapped workers. Such areas as food handling, auto or building maintenance, cleaning and pressing, and light factory work are relatively undeveloped fields.

Bell described a survey of 18 industries covering 2,216 occupations on the unskilled or semiskilled level.[8] It was found that more than half required little or no school training. Some 54 percent of the jobs within the ability of the retarded would not be barred to them by lack of schooling. Of the jobs examined 69 percent required one week or less of on-the-job training to qualify a person.

A more recent study reported by Dr. Milton A. Young [9] again indicates that academic requirements for many kinds of work are low. One hundred and eighteen jobs held by educable retarded persons were analyzed to determine the academic requirements of each one. All job areas required enough skill in reading and writing to fill out an application form. More than 65 percent required about second grade reading and arithmetic, and 85 percent required a little writing and spelling. The more advanced the work, the more academic skills are needed. For example in food preparation the worker might have to read items on the menu, mark containers to go out, and add up a sales slip. The author stresses the importance of using actual job requirements in building a school curriculum.

Operation of most machines demands higher intelligence than the average manual task. The increasing use of machines has barred retarded workers from many opportunities. On the other hand, developing resources for training and placing and serious study of suitable job areas mean that while some fields are closing, others are opening.

Changing economic conditions affect retarded workers as they do all others. In good times the demand for labor is high and there may be jobs for many. In bad times when unemployment is general, the mentally retarded may lose positions. Improved services for teaching, training, and placing, and more recognition of personal factors have already shown that this need not always be the case.

[8] Howard M. Bell, *Matching Youth and Jobs.* (American Council on Education, Washington, D.C.).

[9] "Academic Requirements of Jobs Held by the Educable Retarded in the State of Connecticut." *American Journal of Mental Deficiency* (March, 1958).

Common sense dictates some precautions in placing the retarded in employment. In general, they need work within their ability, mental and physical; work with which they are satisfied; work free from danger; work where they do not endanger others; work where there are not great temptations; and work where employment is not seasonal.

Authorities agree that the lack of judgment, characteristic of mental deficiency, should always be considered in placing them. Driving trucks, for example, an occupation favored by older boys, is obviously not in the public interest. Baby-sitting is just as unsuitable for older girls. Such jobs might be carried successfully for a time, but if even a small emergency arises, a tragedy might result.

Another point stressed is that a good personality often counts more than intelligence in employment. Even good manners and the small amenities of social relations help to get and keep the job.

Training for a limited operation is another accepted principle —a little piece of a job, not a whole trade. A boy may never learn to be an all-round carpenter, but he may be useful in charge of the lumber rack. A girl is not likely to become a chef, yet may find her spot in preparing vegetables.

It is not represented that the successes mentioned above are typical of the whole group. Training for suitable work and skilled help in finding and keeping jobs would obviously go far to offset native limitations. As counseling, vocational training, and job placement become available earlier and to larger numbers, we shall have a better picture of the retarded in the world of work.

XVIII. *The Socializing Process*

WHETHER carried out by the public school, by the home, by the institution, or through community agencies, the ultimate aim of all work with the retarded is socialization—the development of personality in relation to environment so that within the limits of his ability the individual may become a social asset instead of a social liability. This is not different from the aim of all education.

When the mental deficiency problem was conceived of merely in terms of intelligence quotient, or mental age, it did not take on a very hopeful aspect. The I.Q., it was explained, is an index of general native intelligence, which in every individual reaches its full development at a certain chronological age, perhaps not later than sixteen years in the normal person. That is, if the individual, when he had reached the maturity of physical development, had attained a mental age of only nine years, there it seemed his mental age would remain for the rest of his days. All the king's horses and all the king's men could not add one cubit to his stature. So in this strictly intellectual sense, mental deficiency appeared to be a rather hopeless problem.

More recently, some psychological studies have shown gains in I.Q. when the environment has been improved. This reflects the modern concept that the I.Q. indicates the child's operational level, rather than his general intelligence. In some cases a child in very unfavorable circumstances may not be functioning at his highest level. When placed in good surroundings he is able to utilize all of his native capacities. Consequently he scores better on tests. Generally speaking, however, the I.Q. is still regarded as subject to little change throughout life.

The social approach to the problem showed a way out. Could there not be developed by training those qualities, which, even in cases of limited intellects, would enable a number of retarded persons to become useful citizens? This is a question to which the work in homes, the more progressive institutions, public schools, and community agencies has given an affirmative answer. The constructive efforts of these agencies are especially directed toward those elements of personality which have been shown not to be fixed, which are susceptible of improvement, and which are more decisive factors in socialization than intelligence alone. It is well known that in social characteristics, earning ability, and general behavior, retarded persons having the same I.Q. differ markedly: at the one extreme may be found the chronic type of subnormal criminal; at the other extreme of the same mental level may be found the reliable, industrious, respected member of the community.

Obviously, as has already been noted, not all of the mentally deficient are capable of being thus socialized. Some appear to have such unsocial personality trends that to develop their behavior into socially useful or acceptable forms is, with our present knowledge, out of the question. Others receive little or no training until they have reached an age when faulty reactions have become so confirmed that the best efforts cannot overcome them. Such cases represent types for whom indefinite institutional may be required.

Measuring Personal Factors

A number of interesting attempts have been made to distinguish, to define, and even to measure these elements of personality and behavior that make for social success or failure. In 1920, Dr. S. D. Porteus, while serving as director of the department of research of The Training School at Vineland, N.J., published "A Study of Personality of Defectives With a Social Ratings Scale." In this work Dr. Porteus said:

The whole difficulty of the task of test interpretation lies in the fact that behind so-called "mental age" stands the personality of the individual. The psychiatrist is entirely right in his emphasis on the fact that right social adjustment depends upon the whole individual make-up rather than the mentality.

Dr. Porteus described the general qualities affecting social adaptation as follows:

The community into which an individual must fit is, first of all, a working community, hence one of the first things to be determined is the earning capacity. . . . In the next place it is . . . an intelligent working community, so there must be a certain modicum of learning capacity to enable the individual to profit by training and to assimilate ideas. Earning and learning capacity are then closely related to self-support. But even with the ability for self-support, the individual is not fit for the community unless he has also some capacity for self-management and self-control. . . . This capacity for self-management depends mainly upon temperament and disposition, judgment and common sense, whilst self-control must be exhibited in the inhibition of unsocial, instinctive, and impulsive action.[1]

This is the Porteus outline of "factors affecting social fitness":

	1. Earning capacity 2. Learning capacity	Self-support
Social Fitness	3. Temperament and disposition 4. Judgment and common sense	Self-management
	5. Inhibition of antisocial instinct and impulses	Self-control

The components of personality were enumerated in somewhat more detail by Dr. Howard W. Potter, for a number of years Clinical Director at Letchworth Village, one of New York's institutions for the retarded. Dr. Potter said: "When we come to consider the question of the adaptation of mental defectives, we are at once impressed with the fact that those who are not committed to an institution until they approach maturity almost invariably are identified as a result of some behavior or per-

[1] Porteus, No. 23, Publications of the Training School at Vineland, N.J.

sonality disorder. We know further that vast numbers of mental defectives are able to fill a useful niche in the social and economic order. Why is it that one individual is in need of institutional care, while another is able to live satisfactorily in the community? Plainly it is not a matter of intellectual endowment alone. It is, however, a matter of environment and behavior. To understand behavior, we have to consider, among other things, the personality." Dr. Potter defined personality as "the sum of the facilities for adaptation."

Dr. Potter dissected qualities that go to make up personality into eleven principal components as follows: (1) intellectual characteristics; (2) sense of responsibility; (3) industrial efficiency; (4) output of nervous and muscular energy; (5) habitual reactions to inferiority; (6) sociability; (7) conduct and behavior; (8) mood; (9) reactions related to mood; (10) special aptitudes and interests; (11) unique and pathological traits.[2]

A more quantitative method for the measurement of social behavior was the work of Dr. Lloyd N. Yepsen while with the Research Laboratory of The Training School at Vineland. He prepared a Personal Behavior Score Card based on the results of study of the boys and girls at Vineland, and subsequently tested out with other groups. Under various general headings are grouped items of specific personal-social behavior. For example, under the general heading of "Attitude of Others Toward Him," are listed these items for scoring:

> Choose him as a leader.
> Accept him as a leader.
> Seek his companionship.
> Accepted readily as one of group.
> Play with him only occasionally, not often.
> Ignore and shun him.
> Butt of crowd, pick on him.

Since these scales were devised hundreds of personality tests have been developed, but few are well adapted to study of the

[2] Potter, "Personality in Mental Defectives." *Mental Hygiene,* 6:488.

subnormal. Most of them are of the paper and pencil type, in which the retarded are at a disadvantage. Projective techniques, like the Rorschach tests, though requiring verbalization, may be useful if administered by a trained clinician. Sarason [3] points out that projective techniques have shown that behavior of the mentally retarded is not always explained by the I.Q. Case studies are widely used to shed light on personality. The observations of a skilled social worker on behavior in the home, school, and play setting, are often more helpful than a formal test.

The Fourth Mental Measurements Year Book, published in 1953, indicates clearly how interest has changed from intellectual to personality factors. In 1917 when a survey was made of the whole field of psychological tests, there was only one division among tests: references to the Binet-Simon, and references to all other tests, most of which were intelligence tests. In the 1953 Year Book, all intelligence tests combined comprise less than one-fourth of the total of 4,417 references.

In 1935 Dr. Edgar A. Doll, then Director of Research at the Vineland Training School, formulated a method of measuring various aspects of social development. The scale, called the Vineland Social Maturity Scale, was later revised and standardized on normal subjects. It is intended to measure such qualities as social responsibility, independence, and initiative. Levels of performance are indicated through various components of social behavior. The categories include self-help, self-direction, occupation, communication, locomotion, and social relations. It has been shown that such aspects of self-expression mature through various stages which distinguish one age level from another.

Dr. Doll describes the scale as consisting of 117 items which reflect stages in social development from birth to the prime of life. A table converts total scores to equivalent social age values. His 1953 book, *The Measurement of Social Competence*, contains a manual on examination procedure as well as case studies. The extracts below illustrate the method:

[3] Sarason, *Psychological Problems in Mental Deficiency*.

Self help, dressing
  Year 1– 2 Pulls off socks
        2– 3 Removes coat or dress
        3– 4 Buttons coat or dress
        4– 5 Dresses self except for tying

       12–15 Exercises complete care of dress
Socialization
  Year 0– 1 Reaches for familiar persons
              Demands personal attention
        1– 2 Plays with other children

        3– 4 Plays cooperatively at kindergarten level
              "Performs" for others
        4– 5 Plays competitive exercise games
        5– 6 Plays simple table games

       20–25 Assumes responsibility beyond own needs
       25–   Shares community responsibility

Dr. Doll states that the scale can be used as: 1) a standard scale of normal development; 2) a measure of individual differences, and hence of extreme deviations; 3) a qualitative index of variation in abnormal subjects; and 4) a measure of improvement following special treatment.

The scale has also been found useful in distinguishing between mental retardation with and without social incompetence. It gives assistance in child guidance and provides a means of evaluating the influence of environment and of handicaps, such as blindness, deafness, or crippling. The term "social maturity" is used in a limited sense, and does not refer to the degree of socialization or stability.

The Development of Social Behavior

How far it is possible to change personality by conscious effort is a question. From work that has been done in the field of mental hygiene for children, it has been shown that if the child can be reached young enough there is much that can be done at least to aid the personality to *develop* in the right direction by fostering constructive motivation, attitudes and reactions. Dr.

Frank Lorimer believes that advances in biochemistry, genetics, and psychology are beginning to provide the basis for more accurate appraisal of hereditary factors in personality development, as well as in intelligence. Even if the qualities that go to make up personality are regarded as innate and unchangeable, it is apparent from work already done that it is possible to change the manifestations of personality in behavior, which is, after all, the thing with which we are concerned.

Behavior is the product of the interaction of two factors—personality and environment. The process of socializing the retarded may be described as that of so modifying or controlling the environmental stimuli in relation to the personality as to induce the desired responses in behavior. This is in a sense a trial-and-error process until the particular group of environmental stimuli are found which bring the sought-for result. It is a matter of converting these favorable responses into habitual responses that will be stabilized in desirable behavior and outlook.

The term environment is here used in its broadest sense to include the entire group of external stimuli acting upon the individual, as for example, family and friends, living conditions, training and education, employment, etc. Environment is the movable, controllable element which can be brought to bear upon personality in such a way as to effect significant changes in behavior. This is the essence of the work being done in the socialization of the retarded.

The home is considered by all authorities to be the chief factor in determining personality. The impress of parents upon their children is paramount in the early years of life—the most malleable period—when personality traits are being formed. In the home, retarded children, like normal ones, are subject to good or bad influences according to the character and wise or unwise management of parents. The retarded often have less opportunity than average children for wholesome personality development because many of them have inferior home environments. Here the support of positive outside influence is needed, as from the neighborhood house, the welfare agency, the school, the church.

It is believed that social learning derives chiefly from the environment of family and friends, including the play group. The patterns of learning extend from food habits to sex behavior. Even motivation is probably learned. These considerations lead us again to the importance of evaluating the pressures of home, neighborhood, and school, since they largely determine how the individual functions.

The public school is a major socializing force. Regular hours, the discipline of study, group activities, success in achievement of goals, all help to develop social qualities. On one hand conformity to group behavior is required, while on the other hand there is encouragement for initiative, steady growth of interests, and increasing responsibility for self-management.

In many of the cases committed to institutions because of antisocial conduct in the community, the undesired behavior disappears soon after they are received in the institution and removed from conditions that incited the faulty behavior.

The progressive institution begins the socializing process and continues it through to extra-institutional programs such as colonies, family care, parole and, so far as warranted, discharge.

The process of socializing the retarded resolves itself, as does any process of assimilation or socialization, into a matter of *rapprochement* between diverse social elements, in this case the more constructive elements of the community on the one hand, and the mentally deficient on the other. We have seen how the training of these mentally limited persons is directed toward bringing their actions into conformity with social standards. Let us see in what ways society must adapt itself to the mentally deficient.

The Role of Society

Mental defectives, especially until they reach manhood and womanhood, are notably impressionable and easily influenced. That is why they so often fail in a poor environment and cause little or no trouble in a good environment. In short, the mentally deficient quite truly reflect in their behavior the kind of environment in which they find themselves. In that way they are an index of social conditions. If the community finds large numbers of delinquent, socially inadequate defectives in its midst, let it look at itself and ask: "What kind of community have we here, what kinds of homes, schools, neighborhoods, and recreational opportunities?" The trouble must be sought somewhere beyond the subnormal, who may be perpetrators but who rarely are instigators.

How commonly has the attitude of the community toward the mentally deficient been one of social ostracism! Those who by reason of delinquency have come to public notice have usually been regarded as hopelessly bad characters. "Get rid of them; keep them out of our midst," was the usual social reaction. The result of this tendency to cast off the retarded was simply to foster in them those antisocial proclivities with which they have been charged. Such a policy of ostracism, far from solving the problem of mental deficiency, only aggravates it.

How can society best face this problem? By adapting itself to the mentally handicapped to the extent of giving them helpful and practical training and supervision, and by making the community so far as possible safe for those who remain in it.

Will the mentally handicapped repay such efforts on the part of society? There is ample evidence that they will. Among many there is an almost pitiable craving for respectability, an ardent desire to conform, to be like other people, to live, and dress, and play like them, to associate with them, to have their esteem, to be "regular folks." Though inferior in intellect, they have the same emotional drives as others of average or superior intelligence.

The well-organized community as a matter of social expediency will put itself in a position to know its weaker members at as early a period in their lives as possible. It will determine what measures may be instrumental in enabling these individuals to become satisfactorily functioning members of the group. In other words, the far-seeing community will recognize the vast social and economic advantage of authorizing such expenditures for the care of the mentally deficient as may be necessary in making social efficients of the largest possible number. If we may judge by work already done, there will be a profitable measure of success.

XIX. *The Mentally Retarded in the Social Order*

THERE can be no doubt that there are large numbers of adult persons in this country who have mental ages of less than thirteen years, according to the way the intelligence tests measure so-called general intelligence. But from this fact no sound conclusions about the individual's relation to society can be drawn. A mental age of nine, ten, eleven, or twelve years does not, of necessity, imply social inadequacy any more than a mental age which indicates superior intelligence guarantees that that person will not be antisocial. Furthermore, it must not be forgotten that the general intelligence which the tests measure probably does not develop in any one much beyond sixteen years, and that therefore a mental age of eleven, twelve or thirteen, on a scale where the upper limit is sixteen, is not such a great deficiency as might at first appear.

What psychological examinations of large groups of people actually show, is that human intelligence, like other biological and social phenomena, is subject to gradation or distribution, and that this distribution inclines to follow, in general, the lines of the normal frequency curve. In the measurement of intelligence Terman found long ago that the distribution of the intelligence quotients followed closely the normal frequency distribution. What Terman had to say about this distribution is to the point:

Since the frequency of the various grades of intelligence decreases gradually and at no point abruptly on each side of the median, it is evident that there is no definite dividing line between normality and feeblemindedness, or between normality and genius. Psychologically the mentally defective child does not belong to a distinct type, nor does the genius. There is no line of demarcation between either of these extremes and the so-called "normal" child. The number of mentally defective individuals in a population will depend upon the standard arbitrarily set up as to what constitutes mental deficiency.[1]

In psychological research generally, if a large number of individuals selected at random are measured in any given mental trait, the distribution follows that of the normal frequency curve.

There would seem to be nothing, therefore, at which to take alarm in the knowledge we have thus far gained concerning the distribution of human intelligence. It is about as we should have expected from our knowledge of the distribution of other natural

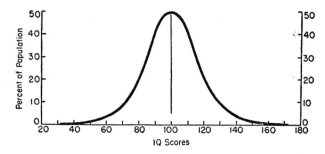

THE NORMAL DISTRIBUTION OF INTELLIGENCE

The graph above was based on tests of school children. Some studies have indicated that the distribution of intelligence may depart somewhat from this balanced curve. Dr. Ernest Gruenberg, when director of an extensive study of retardation in Onondaga County, New York, observed variations from the expected frequencies.

phenomena. The intelligence of the majority of people centers about the mean, and is neither very high nor very low. That makes for stability.

At the same time the intellectual differences in human beings, symmetrically distributed as they are, are basic to social organization and make possible a harmonious social order. It would be a very poor sort of society in a functioning sense which was made up of persons entirely similar in intelligence, in ability, in

[1] Terman, *The Measurement of Intelligence* (Boston, Houghton, 1916).

aptitude. There would be little to make such a society cohere, for the individuals in it would not be mutually interdependent. Cooperation through division of labor is one of the first things essential to the establishment of any social order. Cooperation inheres in the differences which exist among individuals. Were all men created with the intelligence and aptitude of leaders and with the will to lead, the result would not be social organization but social disruption. As Professor C. H. Cooley said:

> The unity of the social mind consists not in agreement but in organization, in the fact of reciprocal influence among its parts, by virtue of which everything that takes place in it is connected with everything else. . . . This differentiated unity of mental or social life, present in the simplest intercourse but capable of infinite growth and adaptation, is what I mean . . . by social organization.[2]

It does not aid in the solution of the problems of retardation merely to deplore the fact that a certain proportion of the human race are of relatively low intelligence. It must be recognized that many of those of lesser intelligence are capable of finding places of usefulness and happiness in the present social order. In fact, it may be said in all truth that many of the intellectually subnormal have a definite, even important, function in society. There are numerous tasks in the world of the routine type that can be well performed day in and day out by the subnormal. Psychological examinations of factory employees have shown, to the employer's surprise, that some of the best operatives are retarded. They are steady, faithful workers who can best stand humdrum toil. A large firm in New York City, after experimenting with its messenger service, came to the conclusion that the retarded youth made the most satisfactory messenger because he was likely to be the most faithful to his duties and was content to hold his position longer than the normal boy. In other studies the same facts have been brought out. Arthur S. Otis in his "The Selection of Mill Workers by Mental Test" tested 300 workers and found no correlation between intelligence and ability to perform the work well. Personnel managers of textile mills took the position that textile mills formerly were operated

<hr>

[2] C. H. Cooley, *Social Organization* (New York, Scribners, 1909), p. 4.

largely by children and therefore they could see no reason why adults with only childlike intelligence should not be able to do perfectly acceptable work. After experimentation it was found that they could.

How the retarded will fare in an automation age remains to be seen. Presumably, they will never be given responsibility for operating expensive machinery. Certainly, however, better training for jobs within their ability and more research on suitable fields of occupation will open hundreds of new opportunities.

The efforts of training agencies are largely directed to paid employment and complete or partial self-support. There is, however, a large proportion of the retarded who can never enter the competitive labor market, yet are very useful at home. An example is a young man with a mental age under six, who by helping his mother enabled her to keep a position as janitress of a building. No longer young, the mother was unable to do heavy work. Under her direction the retarded youth did the hardest of the jobs, he supplying the muscles, she the brains. Hundreds of other retarded young people contribute in some way to the welfare of the home. Training for home duties is beginning to appear in educational programs.

Essential Features of a Program for the Mentally Retarded

Adequate services for the retarded require the participation of many different organizations. Government agencies will carry most of the responsibility but private agencies must share it. The latter include a number of private residential schools.

It is not feasible to suggest, except in general terms, where responsibility should rest for carrying out each part of a satisfactory program. There are great differences in the administrative structure of various states. Among private health and welfare agencies there are wide differences in purpose and resources. Better coordination among organizations is required together with broadening of agency programs more fully to include the retarded.

I. Orientation of those in contact with children (including physicians, nurses, social workers, clergymen, teachers, and parents)
   1. Increased alertness to signs of retardation.
   2. Contact with agencies qualified to diagnose and give early advice to parents.
II. Clinics staffed with appropriate doctors, psychologists, social workers, and therapists
   1. Function:
      a) Complete diagnosis to include physical, mental, educational, and social factors and realistic counsel to parents.
      b) Treatment directed to correcting remediable disorders and developing maximum capacities. Psychotherapy to be included if indicated.
      c) Skilled counseling by clinic social workers in family and community relations.
   2. Extent. If service for mental defectives is included with child guidance, one full-time clinic unit to every 100,000 of population is indicated. If service is for mentally deficient, borderline, and dull normal only, one clinic unit to some 150,000–200,000 of population is indicated.
III. Community Programs
   1. Specialized nursery schools and kindergartens for preschool children living at home.
   2. Day care training centers for those of school age who for special reasons are not in school.
   3. Counseling services for parents and others.
   4. Social service to aid in family problems and adjustment in the community.
IV. School Programs
   1. Function. Program organized according to needs of children whether educable or trainable. To include habit and social training; realistic occupational preparation and guidance; cooperation with vocational training and employment agencies.

2. Extent. Special classes for at least 2 percent of elementary school register. Additional classes for the trainable.
3. Social Service. In cooperation with community agencies, while in school and after leaving school.

V. Vocational Training and Placement
1. Workshops. To provide for social as well as occupational training.
2. Job finding. To include necessary supervision.
3. Exploration of suitable work opportunities.

VI. Community Facilities Adapted to Adults
1. Residence centers for those without suitable homes.
2. Health centers. Provisions for continuing health care.
3. Recreational opportunities.
4. Social service.

VII. Professional and Lay Education
1. Professional groups:
   a) In latest knowledge concerning retardation coming from practice and research.
   b) In methods of counseling parents.
2. Lay groups:
   a) Parents and foster parents in best methods of care and training and planning for the future.
   b) Public in attitude for the mentally deficient and necessity for making proper provision for them.
   c) Public officials in needs requiring public action and appropriation.

VIII. State Institutional Programs
1. Function. To provide for a carefully selected group of the retarded of all ages who, because of special needs or problems, require, for shorter or longer periods, more intensive treatment, training, or care than can be given in home, school, or community.
2. Objective. Social development and return to the community whenever indicated.
3. Extent. Accommodations, with adequate staff, for at least 0.1 percent of total population.

4. Residential treatment units for those with severe emotional or behavior problems, including defective delinquents.
5. Social Service staff skilled in aiding individual's social adjustment both in the institution and in the process of return to the community. Wide use of community facilities.
6. Day classes at institutions for children in community.
7. Colony or half-way houses for care and training.

IX. State Extra-Institutional Program
1. Central Bureau:
   a) To maintain uniform policy on admissions to institutions.
   b) To determine need for admission in individual cases.
   c) To refer to cooperating local agencies children not requiring institutional care.
   d) Home training.
   e) Service to children on waiting lists and their families in cooperation with local agencies.
   f) To aid development of community services for children living at home.
   g) To set standards for community services.
2. Intermediate care:
   a) Family care, supervision, and job placement.

X. Research
1. On causes, prevention, treatment.
2. In educational and social programs.
3. In vocational training and opportunities.
4. In effectiveness of community programs.
5. In cultural factors.

The Retarded Are People

In the growth of a country-wide program for the retarded we may note encouraging changes in emphasis. Roughly, the period 1850–1900 marked the development of institutions. The period from 1900–1950 saw the development of special classes in the public schools and of intelligence and personality tests. The period beginning in 1950 already shows an emphasis on research and a rapid rise of community resources. The organized activities of parents of retarded children have accelerated both these movements and have aided in securing federal grants and programs which before this had been handled almost entirely on a state level.

As we have seen, the very nature of the distribution of human intelligence means that inevitably there will always be, as there always have been, leaders and followers in the social procession. Because some men react to the situation about them more quickly, more completely, and more effectively than others, they become leaders and those who react less adequately become followers. The kind of leadership conducive to social progress is the leadership of those who, combining the best intellectual endowment with the broad-visioned type of social personality, react in the most socially effective ways.

Those of limited intelligence will reflect more closely than other elements of the population the kind of social leadership given them. They are almost entirely dependent upon leadership and *some* kind of leadership they *will* find. In the absence of strong leadership of the right kind, many will gravitate toward the wrong kind and become social liabilities. On the other hand, the retarded may be expected to be among the most faithful followers of a society that sufficiently recognizes their special need for social development and guidance.

The justification for all that has been written here is, that the large group of persons whom we call mentally deficient constitute no small part of the social order. It does not aid in the solution of the problems connected with their presence in society merely to call attention to the problems they present, to say that democracy is a "delusion" because all persons do not have the mental capacity to go through college or even grade school. Progress will be made only by facing the facts and coming to know and understand the retarded in such a way as to make them, to the largest degree possible, social assets instead of social liabilities.

Some pages back we spoke of differences among individuals in such matters as intelligence, ability, and aptitude as being basic to social organization. Along with these necessary differentiations, there must also be a fundamental basis of unity, a large degree of likemindedness if a real society is to exist. Where will such a unity, where will such a basis for likemindedness, be found among individuals of such widely diverging degrees of intelligence as we have seen to exist in the population? That fundamental basis of likemindedness can be found apparently only in an element or elements which may be possessed in more or less equal measure by all regardless of intelligence. That common bond of unity is undoubtedly to be found in the realm of ideals, for the moving power of ideals is connected not so much with intelligence as with the instinctive and emotional make-up of the whole personality. Many of the retarded, as has been shown, are distinctly capable of absorbing ideals and, with a reasonable degree of guidance and encouragement, of living up to them. Those who are concerned about social progress will take special thought for the mentally deficient and in addition to affording them treatment, training, and guidance, will see to it that they also come to hold as a very part of their nature those social ideals which are the means of binding people together in a common society.

In *Little Dorrit* Dickens gives a description of a mentally deficient individual, which, though written long ago, is in striking accord with the modern understanding of such persons. Dickens' description of Maggy not only implies very distinctly the idea of mental age, but also makes clear the ability of the retarded with proper training and supervision, to become self-supporting, respected members of the community. Maggy's guardian, Little Dorrit, explains that "When Maggy was ten years old, she had a bad fever, sir, and she has never grown any older ever since."

Although Maggy's mental age was thus fixed at a fairly low level, she continued to develop in other ways under Little Dorrit's sympathetic guidance, to such an extent that she came to fill a useful place in the social order. To continue Little Dorrit's history: "At length in course of time, Maggy began to take pains to improve herself, and to be very attentive and very industrious;

Selected Bibliography

Books and Periodicals

American Journal of Mental Deficiency

Barr, M. W. Mental Defectives: Their Treatment and Training. Philadelphia, Blackiston, 1904.

Children Limited

Crutcher, Hester B. Foster Home Care for Mental Patients. Cambridge, Harvard University Press and the Commonwealth Fund, 1944.

Culver, Magnolia G. Family Care. Columbus, Ohio, Division of Mental Health, 1947.

Di Michael, Salvatore, ed. Vocational Rehabilitation of the Mentally Retarded. U.S. Government Printing Office, 1950. Reprinted in *American Journal of Mental Deficiency*, October, 1952.

Doll, Edgar A. Measurement of Social Competence. Philadelphia, Educational Test Bureau, 1953.

Gesell, Arnold. The Retarded Child: How to Help Him. Bloomington, Ill., Public School Publishing Co., 1925.

Healy, William and Augusta Bronner. New Light on Delinquency. New Haven, Yale University Press, 1936.

Glueck, Sheldon and Eleanor Glueck. Delinquents in the Making. Cambridge, Harvard University Press and the Commonwealth Fund, 1952.

―――― Unraveling Juvenile Delinquency. Cambridge, Harvard University Press and the Commonwealth Fund, 1950.

Hill, Arthur S. The Forward Look—The Severly Handicapped Child Goes to School. U.S. Government Printing Office, 1952.

Journal of Exceptional Children. National Educational Association, 1949.

Journal of Mental Deficiency Research. Publication office: 10 Sheridan Way, Seven Oaks, Kent, England.

Kirk, Samuel A. and G. Orville Johnson. Educating the Retarded Child. New York, Houghton Mifflin, 1951.

Martens, Elsie H. Curriculum Adjustments for the Mentally Retarded. U.S. Government Printing Office, 1950.

Penrose, Lionel S. The Biology of Mental Defect. New York, Grunde and Stratton and Sidgwick and Jackson, 1945.

Pines, Maya and Cornell Capa. Retarded Children Can Be Helped. Great Neck, N.Y., Channel Press, 1957.

Pollock, Horatio M. Family Care of Mental Patients. Utica State Hospital Press, 1936.

Proceedings of Conferences of the Woods Schools. Langhorne, Pa. Published yearly.

Sarason, Seymour B. Psychological Problems in Mental Deficiency. 2d ed. New York, Harper, 1953.

Seguin, Edouard. Idiocy: And Its Treatment by the Physiological Method. Educational Reprint #2. Teachers College, Columbia University, 1907.

Stern, Curt. Principles of Human Genetics. San Francisco, W. H. Freeman, 1949.

Tredgold, R. F. and K. Soddy. Textbook of Mental Deficiency. 9th ed. Baltimore, Williams and Wilkins, 1956.

Directories

Directory for Exceptional Children:
Schools, Services, Other Facilities. Boston, Porter Sargent, 1958. Revised periodically.

Handbook. Appendix A. American Association on Mental Deficiency. P.O. Box 96, Willimantic, Conn. Listing of public and private schools for the mentally retarded, 1958. Revised biennially. Price: $1.00.

Psychiatric Clinics and Other Resources in the U.S. National Institute of Mental Health, 1956. Price: $1.25. Revised at intervals.

Pamphlets

The organizations below furnish free reading lists on request, and pamphlets at cost price on many aspects of retardation.

National Association for Mental Health, 10 Columbus Circle, NYC 19, N.Y.

National Association for Retarded Children, 99 University Place, NYC 3, N.Y.

U.S. Children's Bureau, Washington, D.C.

Permissions

THE author is indebted to the following publishers, periodicals, organizations, and individuals for their cooperation in making available much valuable material:

The *American Breeders Magazine*, for the article "Heredity in Feeblemindedness"; the American Council on Education, for Howard M. Bell's *Matching Youth and Jobs*; the American Eugenics Society, for Laughlin's *Eugenical Sterilization*; the *American Journal of Mental Deficiency* and Richard H. Hungerford and the *Journal of Psycho-Aesthenics*, for the many articles cited throughout; the *American Journal of Psychiatry*, for Neil A. Dayton's "Order of Birth and Size of Family"; Blackiston, Philadelphia, for M. W. Barr's *Mental Defectives: Their Treatment and Training*; the *Boston Medical and Surgical Journal*, for V. V. Anderson's "Feeblemindedness As Seen in Court"; reports of the British Royal Commission; the Carnegie Institute, New York, for Arthur H. Estabrook's *The Jukes in 1915*; the Channel Press, Great Neck, N.Y., for Maya Pines and Cornell Capa's *Retarded Children Can Be Helped*; the Children's Bureau, Washington, D.C.; the Columbus, Ohio Division of Public Health, for Magnolia G. Culver's *Family Care*; *Contemporary Review*; the Department of Health, Education, and Welfare, for "Vocational Rehabilitation of the Mentally Retarded"; Dodd, Mead of New York, for permission to reprint material from H. H. Goddard's *Psychology of the Normal and Subnormal*

The Educational Test Bureau, Minneapolis, for Edgar A. Doll's work on the Social Maturity Scale; *Eugenical News*, for the article "Trends in Capacity for Intelligence"; Eugenics Records, for Davenport and Danielson's *The Hill Folk*; the Government Printing Office, for Arthur S. Hill's "The Forward Look: The Severely Handicapped Child"; Maurice H. Fouracre of Teachers College, Columbia University, New York; Freeman and Company, San Francisco, for Curt Stern's *Principles of Human Genetics*; Grune and Stratton, New York, and Sidgwick and Jackson, for Lionel S. Penrose's *Biology of Mental Defect*; Edward C. Harold and Katharine F. Hope, for "Employment of Patients Discharged from the St. Louis State Training School"; Harpers, New York, for Seymour B. Sarason's *Psychological Problems in Mental Deficiency;* Harvard University Press, Cambridge, for Hester B. Crutcher's *Foster Care of Mental Patients* and Sheldon and Eleanor Glueck's *Unraveling Juvenile Delinquency,* which are quoted with the permission of the publishers and the Commonwealth Fund; Henry Holt, New York, for Charles B. Davenport's *Heredity in Relation to Eugenics;* Houghton Mifflin, Boston, for L. M. Terman's *The Measurement of Intelligence*

The Jarvis School for Boys, Toronto, for the study "Follow-up of 1,000 Non-Academic Boys"; G. Orville Johnson of Syracuse University; the *Journal of Exceptional Children;* the Journal Press, Provincetown, Mass., for Don C. Charles' "Ability and Accomplishments of Persons Earlier Judged Mentally Deficient," printed in *Genetic Psychology Monographs;* the Judge Baker Foundation Publications, Boston, for William Healy and Augusta Bronner's *Delinquents and Criminals: Their Making and Unmaking;* Longmans, Green, New York, for R. J. Fynne's *Montessori and Her Inspirers;* Macmillan, New York, for H. H. Goddard's *Feeblemindedness: Its Causes and Consequences* and *The Kallikak Family;* the Mansfield and Southbury Training Schools, Connecticut; the Massachusetts State School for the Feebleminded; *Mental Hygiene,* for Walter E. Fernald's "Standardized Fields of Inquiry for Clinical Studies of Borderline Defectives," Bernard Glueck's "Concerning Prisoners," and Henry Potter's "Personality in Mental Defectives"; *Mental Welfare,* for A. F. Tredgold's "Sterilization of Mental Defectives"

National Conference Charities and Correction, for Walter E. Fernald's "History of the Treatment of the Feebleminded"; National Conference of Juvenile Agencies, Jackson, Miss., for Fred O. Butler's "Sterilization Procedure and Its Success in California"; the National Association of Social Workers, for Jean Weidensall's *Mentality of the Unmarried Mother;* the Newark State School, Newark, N.J., for Fisher and Wolfson's "Group Therapy of Mental Defectives"; the New York State Interdepartmental Mental Health Resources Board; *Occupational Education;* the Pacific Colony of Spada, Cal.; Public School Publishing Co., Bloomington, Ill., for Arnold Gesell's *The Retarded Child: How to Help Him;* Putnam, New York, for Richard L. Dugdale's *The Jukes;* the Rome State School, N.Y.; Scribners, New York, for C. H. Cooley's *Social Organization;* the State Charities Aid Association, for Anne Moore's *The Feebleminded in New York;* Harry C. Storrs and George A. Jervis of Letchworth Village, N.Y.; *The Survey,* for Walter C. Fernald's "The Templeton Farm Colony for the Feebleminded"; the Syracuse State School; Teachers College, Columbia University, for Edouard Seguin's *Idiocy and Its Treatment by the Physiological Method;* The Training School, Vineland, N.J., for Binet and Simon's *The Development of Intelligence in Children*

Utica State Hospital Press, for Horatio M. Pollock's *Family Care of Mental Patients;* Williams and Wilkins, Baltimore, for A. Myerson's *Inheritance of Mental Diseases* and A. F. Tredgold and K. Soddy's *Textbook of Mental Deficiency;* Wood, New York, for A. F. Tredgold's *Mental Deficiency;* World, New York, for H. H. Goddard's *School Training of Defective Children;* the World Health Organization for L. Bovet's "Psychiatric Aspects of Juvenile Delinqency"; and Yale University Press, New Haven, Conn., for William Healy and Augusta Bronner's *New Light on Delinquency.*

Index